FABER has published children's books since 1929. T. S. Eliot's *Old Possum's Book of Practical Cats* and Ted Hughes's *The Iron Man* were amongst the first. Our catalogue at the time said that 'it is by reading such books that children learn the difference between the shoddy and the genuine'. We still believe in the power of reading to transform children's lives. All our books are chosen with the express intention of growing a love of reading, a thirst for knowledge and to cultivate empathy. We pride ourselves on responsible editing. Last but not least, we believe in kind and inclusive books in which all children feel represented and important.

Writer and historian David Long is the award-winning and bestselling author of the acclaimed Survivors series, *Pirates Magnified*, *We are the Romans*, *The World's Most Magnificent Machines*, *Tragedy at Sea*, *The Story of the London Underground* and more than twenty other non-fiction books on a wide range of historical subjects. He is married to Rosy and lives in Suffolk.

Terri Po is a children's book illustrator who was highly commended in the FAB Prize. She is originally from Hong Kong but graduated from the University of Edinburgh in 2018. She creates editorial illustrations, infographics and illustrated books, as well as doing live graphic facilitation.

First published in the UK in 2024
First published in the US in 2024
by Faber & Faber Limited
The Bindery, 51 Hatton Garden
London EC1N 8HN
faber.co.uk

Typeset by Faber in Mr Eaves
This font has been specially chosen to support reading

Printed and bound in Latvia

All rights reserved
Text © David Long, 2024
Illustrations © Terri Po, 2024

The right of David Long and Terri Po to be identified as author and illustrator respectively
of this work has been asserted in accordance with Section 77 of the Copyright,
Designs and Patents Act 1988

*This book is sold subject to the condition that it shall not, by way of trade or otherwise, be lent,
resold, resold, hired out or otherwise circulated without the publisher's prior consent in any
form of binding or cover other than that in which it is published that in which it is published and
without a similar condition including this condition being imposed on the subsequent purchaser*

A CIP record for this book is available from the British Library

ISBN 978-0-571-37479-3

Printed and bound on FSC® paper in line with our continuing commitment

to ethical business practices, sustainability and the environment.

For further information see faber.co.uk/environmental-policy

2 4 6 8 10 9 7 5 3 1

For my parents, who gave us all wings.

CONTENTS

Introduction – The Dream of Flight	1
Brother Elmer – Trusting a Pair of Home-Made Wings (England, Eleventh Century)	5
A Sheep, a Cockerel and a Duck – The First Passengers (France, 1783)	11
George Cayley – 'I'm Too Old to Fly, Send That Child Up Instead' (England, 1849)	17
Ferdinand von Zeppelin – The World's First Passenger Airline (Germany, 1900)	23
The Wright Brothers – The First Real Aeroplane (US, 1903)	29
Louis Blériot – Crossing the English Channel (France–England, 1909)	35
Dogfight – Aeroplanes Go into Battle (Mexico, 1913)	41
Katherine Stinson – Looping the Loop in a Flying Circus (US, 1915)	47
Queen Bess – The First Black Woman Pilot (France, 1921)	53
Alan Cobham – To Australia and Back Again (1926)	59

Charles Lindbergh – Alone Above the Atlantic (Atlantic Ocean, 1927)   67

Seaplanes – The Need for Speed (Italy, 1927)   73

The TsAGI 1-EA – The First Helicopter Lifts Off (Russia, 1932)   79

Douglas Douglas-Hamilton – A Daring Flight Over Everest (Nepal, 1933)   85

Amelia Earhart – Vanishing Without a Trace (Pacific Ocean, 1937)   91

Empire C-Class – Crash of a Flying Giant (Belgian Congo, 1939)   97

The Attagirls – 'I Flew 400 Spitfires' (UK, 1940)   105

Night Witches – The First Female Fighter Pilots (Russia, 1941)   111

Colditz Cock – An Incredible Escape Attempt (Germany, 1944)   117

Lothar Sieber – The Tragic Human Firework (Germany, 1945)   125

Chuck Yeager – Flying Faster Than a Bullet (US, 1947)   131

The de Havilland Comet – The Beginning of the Jet Age (UK, 1952)   137

Gary Powers – Spies in the Sky (US, 1956)   143

Yuri Gagarin – The First Man in Space (Russia, 1961)   151

Alan Pollock – A Birthday Surprise for London (England, 1968) 157

Concorde – Fast, Faster, Fastest (UK/France, 1969) 163

The Saturn V Rockets – Walking on the Moon (Outer Space, 1969) 169

The Northrop-Grumman B-2 Spirit – Now You See Us, Now You Don't (US, 1977) 177

SpaceShipOne – Joyrides to the Stars (US, 2003) 183

Epilogue – Going Green 189

Introduction

The Dream of Flight

For thousands of years humans have wanted to fly like birds, and almost every country in the world and every culture has its own myths and legends about doing so. Storytellers have woven colourful tales of angels and devils in the skies above our heads. Children have been fascinated by adventures involving flying carpets and fiery golden chariots. Famous artists have created sculptures and paintings of heroic figures swooping down from the clouds, often on the backs of winged horses, dragons or serpents.

Today flying in an aeroplane is something millions of people do every day. Many passengers travel this way so often that they take it for granted. They never stop to wonder how a jet manages to climb so high or fly so fast. They don't think about the early pioneers and the bravery of the men and women who were prepared to risk their lives in simple contraptions that they had designed and built themselves at home. Some miss the wonderful opportunity to gaze out of the window at the magical view of our planet down below.

Enjoying a bird's-eye view of the world is a treat, but perhaps the most amazing thing is the breathtaking pace at which aircraft and other flying machines have been developed to fly faster, higher and further than ever before.

In 1903 Wilbur and Orville Wright became **the first people ever** to pilot an aeroplane. The Wright brothers' initial flight lasted only twelve seconds before their simple wooden-framed device bumped back down to the ground just 37 metres from where it had taken off. A mere sixteen years later another two men flew more than 3,000 kilometres across the Atlantic non-stop, and by 1969 three American astronauts had successfully flown more than 380,000 kilometres between take-off and landing. That's approximately ten million times further than the Wright brothers had travelled. Their rocket had taken them to the Moon and back and enabled two of them to walk on its surface.

Few technologies have ever progressed so far over the course of a single person's lifetime, and yet, as the incredible true adventures in this book demonstrate, the history of flight is not just a story about ever better machinery. It's also about the courage and ingenuity of the men and women (and, in one extraordinary case, a ten-year-old child) who made it possible to progress so rapidly. Finally, and perhaps most of all, it's about the thrilling realisation of a dream that had both fascinated and frustrated so many human beings over so many thousands of years.

Although this urge to fly like a bird is almost as old as mankind itself, most of the early

attempts ended in disaster, and more than a few resulted in the deaths of those adventurers who had decided to risk all and give it a go. Many of these people had been inspired by an ancient Greek legend about an inventor called Daedalus. He constructed two pairs of wings out of candlewax and feathers and strapped the first set on to his back as part of a daring escape from the Mediterranean island of Crete. The second pair was for his son, Icarus, who was imprisoned with him on the island.

Daedalus warned Icarus not to fly too close to the Sun, saying that the heat would melt the wax and cause all the feathers to fall out. Unfortunately, the teenager found flying around so much fun that he immediately forgot everything his father had just told him. His beautiful angel's wings began to fall apart as soon as the wax warmed up, and poor old Icarus `dropped into the sea and drowned`.

In fact, even if Daedalus and Icarus were real people, it probably wouldn't have happened like this at all, because the air actually gets cooler, not warmer, as one flies higher and higher. Despite this (and the story's disastrous ending), the pair became world famous and their story continued to excite and inspire many more flyers in the centuries that followed.

Brother Elmer

Trusting a Pair of Home-Made Wings
(England, Eleventh Century)

A monk from Malmesbury in Wiltshire was possibly the first person in England to try flying. He was called Elmer*, and by the Middle Ages people like him had begun to realise that home-made wings might not be enough to fly like a bird.

Birds are much smaller and lighter than humans, but they have relatively large chest muscles, which they use to control their wings. Even when it became possible to construct a pair of large wings that could move up and down, no human had the strength needed to flap them with enough force to take off and fly.

One answer to this problem, Elmer thought, might be to use a set of home-made wings and simply glide down to the ground from somewhere higher up. It wasn't quite the same thing as flying but it was better than nothing, and several adventurers thought it was worth a try.

---

* Although I call him Elmer, he may actually have been named Oliver – historians aren't sure which.

Church steeples and towers were the tallest things most people had ever seen in the Middle Ages. They were bigger than many trees, and the towers usually had a narrow spiral staircase going right up to the top. A lot of them also had a flat roof, which must have looked like the perfect launch pad for anyone who was thinking of jumping off.

We know about Elmer only because another monk called William wrote an important book about life in medieval Britain. Happily for us, it contains a brief description of Elmer's flight and some information about the man himself.

William's book describes him as a very old man and says that when he was a boy he loved hearing ancient legends about people who could fly. He believed they were true and decided that one day he would try making some wings of his own to see if he could fly like the Greeks.

Unfortunately, William didn't know much about the wings' design or even what they were made of. However, he says that when they were completed, Elmer attached them to his feet as well as to his hands, and that after `jumping off the tower` he managed to glide for about 200 metres before reaching the ground.

According to William, Elmer had chosen a windy day for his adventure. He might have thought that a slight breeze would help him glide even further, but instead he experienced some turbulence on the way down. William calls this 'swirling air' and says that as a result,

Elmer crashed into the ground and broke both his legs. The old monk survived the fall, although he walked with a limp for the rest of his life.

Elmer always blamed himself for the crash. He later said he should have made a tail to go with the wings. However, because he never tried to fly again, he was unable to prove whether he was right or wrong about this.

In the following centuries several other people performed similar feats of daring, in Asia as well as in Europe. Sometimes these involved home-made wings, but a few different ideas were tried out as well. In the thirteenth century, for example, the explorer Marco Polo described a Chinese attempt to fly that involved strapping someone to a sort of kite. In seventeenth-century Turkey a man called Hezârfen Ahmed Çelebi is said to have glided even further than Elmer managed. Afterwards he was given a large bag of gold coins as a reward for his successful landing, but again we can't be completely sure about this. It may just be a myth.

Çelebi's brother Lagari apparently went on to try something that sounds even more dangerous: he strapped himself to a primitive rocket. This was really just a very large firework, but Lagari somehow survived when it eventually crashed into the sea.

The Italian artist and inventor Leonardo da Vinci was also interested in flying, although his ideas sound a lot safer than Legari's. This was probably because he was one of the first people to think scientifically about how to get an actual machine to fly rather than just trying to copy the birds.

Da Vinci spent many hours studying the science of flight, in the way that modern engineers do now. He went on to design several fascinating-looking machines, and although he didn't get around to building any of them, his drawings and plans were highly detailed and are still studied by people today.

Da Vinci's ideas were complex and very clever. They included a machine called an ornithopter, which had flapping wings, and a large, spiral-shaped device, which was designed to spin fast enough to wind itself up into the air. However, both were far too complicated for anyone to build during da Vinci's own lifetime, and when he died in 1519 there was still no practical way of powering them.

A Sheep, a Cockerel and a Duck

The First Passengers (France, 1783)

Finding enough power to fly was still a problem in the eighteenth century. The newly invented steam engine was powerful, but it was much too heavy, and by this time nearly everyone agreed that human muscle-power wasn't going to work either. Humans just weren't strong enough to provide sufficient power, and so people began experimenting with completely different ideas that didn't involve wings at all.

One of the most intelligent came from two French brothers, Joseph-Michel and Jacques-Étienne Montgolfier. Joseph-Michel later claimed he had been gazing at a fireplace in his home when he noticed how smoke and sparks from the burning wood always drifted upwards. He found this curious, especially when he filled a small bag made of thin silk with smoke from the fire and it too floated up into the air.

At first he and his brother thought the burning wood must be giving off a mysterious gas that filled the bag and made it float upwards. They continued experimenting and soon discovered that the same thing happened when the bag was filled with heated air instead of smoke. The brothers didn't know that air expands as it heats up. This means that warm air is less dense than cold air, and their experiments showed that the difference was enough to make a bag rise upwards.

The pair were fascinated by this phenomenon and started making balloons instead of bags, beginning with small ones and then gradually increasing their size. The first few were made of paper because the Montgolfier family owned a paper factory, but later they started to use fabrics such as linen and silk. These worked even better, although there was no way the brothers could control a balloon once it had started rising. Each one just drifted along with the wind and then sank back to the ground when the air inside started to cool down.

By September 1783 the Montgolfiers had finished building their **largest balloon so far** and were ready to put on a spectacular public demonstration. This new one was 10 metres in diameter and made of a type of pale blue silk called taffeta, which was painted with a special varnish to make it waterproof and protect it from the fire used to heat the air inside. The outside of the balloon was also richly decorated with pictures of a large golden sun. This was a favourite design of the French king, Louis XVI, and his queen, Marie Antoinette.

The brothers wanted very much to impress the royal family with their new invention, so they arranged for the demonstration flight to take place near Versailles, the King's large, luxurious palace outside Paris. News of this exciting event quickly spread through the streets of the city, and on the day of the launch more than 130,000 men, women and children travelled out to the countryside to see what was going on.

At this time no one knew how safe balloons were or if it was even possible for a person to survive if they went more than a few metres up in the air. The King calmly suggested sending two convicted criminals up in the balloon to find out. This way, he seemed to think, it wouldn't matter if they died from lack of oxygen, or through fear, or by falling to the ground.

The Montgolfiers weren't at all sure about this idea and decided to use animals instead. A sheep, a duck and a cockerel were found and all three were placed into a special circular basket slung beneath the great balloon.

The brothers had genuine, scientific reasons for choosing the animals they did. In the eighteenth century the sheep's biology was believed to be very similar to our own. The Montgolfiers assumed the duck would be fine because ducks are used to flying quite high. They also thought the cockerel would make an interesting comparison with the duck because, although both are birds that fly, chickens usually stay quite close to the ground.

Once the animals were in the basket, a straw fire was carefully lit beneath the balloon. As

the air inside it warmed up, the three animals were launched skywards to the sound of loud clapping and cheering from the enormous crowd. The balloon quickly rose more than 450 metres into the sky and then, after being caught by a strong breeze, began to float away quite fast. Hundreds of excited spectators ran after it. The royal couple stayed where they were but, like everyone else, they wanted to find out if the animals would survive when the beautiful blue balloon eventually came back down to earth.

After travelling about 3.5 kilometres, and with the air inside cooling down rapidly, the balloon began drifting closer and closer to the ground. Eight minutes after take-off, it finally landed in a field with a soft thump and promptly collapsed as the air inside it rushed out. Gathering round, the spectators could see at once that `all three animals had survived` their ordeal. The world's first-ever passenger flight had been short and uncontrolled but a complete success.

The excitement surrounding the Montgolfiers' demonstration meant that for a while balloons became wildly popular. All over Europe people started buying souvenir clocks and china cups and saucers covered in pictures of them, and fashionable pieces of furniture were made and sold with balloon-shaped designs carved into the wood.

The first human passengers took to the air in a balloon less than two months after the sheep and the two birds, and this delighted the public even more. Their flight lasted three times longer than the first one, but then an attempt to cross the Channel between England and

14

France **ended in disaster** when the balloon caught fire. A French schoolteacher and his companion were killed in this terrible accident, and when another burning balloon came down in Ireland more than a hundred homes were almost completely destroyed in the resulting fire.

These huge, colourful balloons nevertheless looked spectacular, and despite the occasional disaster crowds of people always gathered to watch whenever an aviator was getting ready to lift off. Not everyone believed that they were the answer, however. The view from a balloon was certainly amazing, but for many this wasn't really flying but merely floating . . .

George Cayley

'I'm Too Old to Fly, Send That Child Up Instead' (England, 1849)

Rival inventors carried on trying to design and build machines that could be properly controlled by a pilot instead of just drifting along in the wind like a balloon. Sir George Cayley, in the north of England, was one of the most successful. Ever since school he had been interested in all sorts of mechanical problems. He loved solving puzzles and later became a talented, hard-working engineer, as well as a Member of Parliament. Somehow he also found time to design a series of different flying machines and come up with some genuinely useful inventions, including a new type of unsinkable lifeboat, special lightweight wheels and the first-ever seat belt.

He also built a small engine that was fuelled by gunpowder, but this was less successful. The noisy little engine weighed a lot less than a normal Victorian steam engine, and Cayley had hoped the exploding gunpowder would give it enough power to move the wings of a flying machine up and down.

Sadly, it didn't, and like others before him, Cayley gradually came to accept that all the available engines were still either underpowered or simply too heavy to fly. Because of this, he decided to switch his attention to gliders, and the results of his experiments were so impressive that he is now regarded as `one of the most important pioneers in the history of manned flight`.

The reason for Cayley's success is that he always took a methodical and highly scientific approach to all his research. As part of his investigations into gliders, for example, he spent many hours watching hundreds of seagulls flying near his home in Yorkshire. He noticed that once the birds were actually airborne, they could fly higher or lower just by changing the angle and shape of their wings as they moved in the wind.

Because getting a machine like an ornithopter to fly by using flapping wings was extremely difficult, maybe even impossible, Cayley was more determined than ever to discover how the seagulls were able fly higher without needing to flap theirs. To help him understand, he started building lots of different model wings and a series of tiny gliders. These looked a bit like paper aeroplanes or toys, but he carefully tested each one. He did this by launching them down the staircase at home when his wife was out of the house.

This was the first time anyone in the world had experimented with gliders, even very small ones, and the experiments taught Cayley that some wing shapes worked much better than others. One important discovery was that curved surfaces made better wings than flat ones.

Another was that some sort of tail was essential, so it seemed that Elmer of Malmesbury had been right after all!

Once Cayley had decided which curved shape worked best, he began to construct a full-sized version of his glider, one which could be tested outside in more realistic conditions. This would have to be large enough and strong enough to carry a pilot, but it also had to be extremely light, like a seagull.

Cayley designed the smooth, pointed body – or fuselage – of the glider to look a bit like a little rowing boat. It was carefully streamlined to slip through the air as easily as possible, in the same way that a boat slips through water. To make it as light as possible it was constructed around a thin wooden frame. A second simple wooden frame supported a huge curved wing above the 'boat'. This was made of a fabric similar to that of a modern kite in order to keep the weight to a minimum. For the same reason, the wheels had spokes made of tightly wound string instead of metal.

This makes Cayley's glider sound like a rather strange, home-made contraption, but in fact he had made a crucial breakthrough. Cayley's invention is now regarded as an important landmark in the history of flying, one which pointed the way to nearly all future aeroplane designs. Although it didn't have an engine, his glider had a body, wings and a tail like a normal, modern aeroplane, as well as the same sort of curved surfaces (known as aerofoils) that enable aircraft to fly.

The inventor's plan was for the finished glider to be pulled down the slope of a steep hill in order to take off, although Cayley had already decided that he wasn't going to get into it himself. This was probably because he thought he was too old to fly (he was at least seventy-five years old by the time the glider was ready in 1849), and not because he thought the whole thing looked rather dangerous.

Instead, he persuaded a young boy to climb on board, and the glider was then towed down the hill into a slight breeze. The boy was only ten years old, but unfortunately no one recorded his name. This is a great shame because historians now believe that this little boy from Yorkshire was the first person to fly in an aeroplane anywhere in the world.

As with the Montgolfiers' balloon, the boy's historic flight didn't last very long at all, but no bones were broken, and so everyone agreed it was a great success. Cayley was certainly pleased with the result, but like most inventors he was always looking for a way to improve things. He spent the next few years working on his theories and building an even better machine. By 1853 he finally had another one ready. This time he was confident it could carry a fully grown adult, so he asked his coachman to take on the job of piloting it.

The servant agreed, and once again the glider was towed down the big hill and into the wind. This time it stayed aloft for several hundred metres, and Cayley was even more delighted than before. The coachman was uninjured, but unlike the schoolboy he was clearly

shaken up by the experience. As soon as he had climbed out of the glider he walked over to his employer and resigned. 'I was hired to drive you,' he said, 'not to fly.'

Sadly, Sir George Cayley died three years later, but inventors in Germany and the US, as well as Britain, continued to build gliders of their own. The old man from Yorkshire had shown them what an aircraft needed in order to fly, and now they set out to improve and refine some of his brilliant ideas.

Over the course of about five years one of them, a German pilot called Otto Lilienthal, managed hundreds of successful flights in his gliders. During many of these he flew several hundred metres into the air, much higher than Cayley's coachman had done, and stayed up for much longer.

Ferdinand von Zeppelin

```
The World's First Passenger Airline
          (Germany, 1900)
```

The main problem with nineteenth-century aircraft was that engines at this time were still very unsophisticated compared to the ones we have today. Even if they could take off – and most couldn't – they weren't at all reliable. And while gliders were definitely becoming more advanced aerodynamically, they could still carry only one person. Because of this, some aviators began looking again at lighter-than-air machines, like the Montgolfiers' balloons.

Count Ferdinand von Zeppelin was a German aristocrat who preferred balloons to gliders, especially a new type called an airship. He became even more convinced about this when Otto Lilienthal died after his glider crashed to the ground, breaking his back.

Von Zeppelin's designs for airships looked like long, cylindrical-shaped balloons, but they had metal frames inside them and were filled with hydrogen gas rather than smoke or hot air.

The first prototype he built, called the LZ-1, successfully carried five people more than 400 metres up into the air and then travelled a distance of almost six kilometres before landing safely.

Hydrogen is one of the most inflammable, most explosive substances on Earth, but because it is so light it provides much more lift than hot air or smoke. Storing it is very difficult, however, and to avoid any dangerous leaks the gas in von Zeppelin's airships was held in enormous bags made from the intestines of nearly a quarter of a million cows.

Because an airship filled with hydrogen is so light it can be fitted with quite heavy engines and very large propellers. This means it cans be piloted in a particular direction, instead of just drifting along in the wind like a normal balloon. Even if one of the engines stops working, as one did during that very first flight, the airship will still float in the air instead of plummeting down disastrously like poor old Otto in his glider.

Compared to a glider, airships are gigantic. The LZ-1 was quite a small one, but it was still nearly 130 metres long. When it wasn't flying it was kept in a special floating hangar on Lake Constance (the largest lake in Germany), but von Zeppelin realised that if he built even bigger ones, they could be fitted with even more engines. If one engine out of four failed, it would be less of a problem than if one broke down when there were only two of them. Equipping an airship with multiple engines would also make it possible to travel faster over much greater distances. A bigger airship could carry

many more passengers too – not just a handful like the LZ-1 but dozens or even hundreds.

The count was excited by this idea and saw no reason why the very largest airships couldn't carry passengers thousands of kilometres across the sea. By modern standards their top speed of 130 kilometres an hour doesn't sound very impressive, but they could complete the journey across the Atlantic from Europe to America in two days, less than half the time it took in even the fastest and most advanced new ocean liner.

From now on, each time von Zeppelin built an airship it was even larger than his previous one. When he had completed the fourth he took King Wilhelm II of Württemberg up in it, together with his wife, Queen Charlotte. It quickly set a new world record by flying from Württemberg all the way to Switzerland and back and staying airborne for twelve hours. This achievement, and the news that the count had taken royal passengers up in the LZ-4, made headlines around the world.

All this publicity meant that more and more people wanted to have a go themselves, so in 1910 a new company was formed in the city of Düsseldorf. This was called the Deutsche Luftschiffahrts-Aktiengesellschaft (or the German Airship Travel Corporation), and it was the world's first passenger airline.

Going anywhere in a Zeppelin, however, was very, very expensive. For this reason, the German Airship Travel Corporation was interested in attracting only the very rich. Like the count, it wanted longer and longer airships to accommodate as many of them as possible. Von Zeppelin's new giants of the skies would enable the company to carry everyone who could afford to fly, and to offer them the sorts of comforts and luxuries the very rich expected to enjoy on board an ocean liner.

The count was happy to keep on increasing the size of his machines, and so began work on his greatest creation so far, the LZ-129 *Hindenburg*. This measured 245 metres from end to end, which is longer than ten tennis courts, and it is still the largest flying machine ever built. It contained an incredible 200 million litres of highly explosive hydrogen, and each of its four powerful diesel engines turned a gigantic 5.7-metre wooden propeller.

Accommodation was provided on board for the captain, his crew and a total of seventy-two passengers. This included a shower room and proper bedrooms, as well as a cocktail bar, dining room and comfortable lounge areas. The food was of a very high standard, like in a smart restaurant in Paris or New York, and there was even a dance floor with a grand piano. The piano was made of special lightweight metal covered in pigskin. Surprisingly, there was even a special room where passengers could smoke cigars. This wasn't allowed anywhere else on the *Hindenburg* because of the risk of all that hydrogen exploding.

The gas was held in sixteen vast balloon-like bags, each one much, much larger than a family house. By this time the cattle intestines had been replaced by a special cotton fabric

that was carefully impregnated with chemicals to reduce the risk of leaks as far as possible.

Unfortunately, it was impossible to avoid leaks altogether, and in May 1937 disaster struck as the *Hindenburg* arrived at its landing site in the American state of New Jersey. Cheering crowds of spectators and several film crews had gathered to see the magnificent machine manoeuvring into place overhead, but their noisy excitement suddenly turned to screams of horror as flames were spotted creeping along the airship's huge silvery sides.

Within seconds the entire thing was ablaze, and the world's greatest airship came crashing down to the ground moments later. Many of the passengers were injured while leaping to safety, but more than a dozen were killed, along with twenty-two members of the crew. Horrifying film of the disaster was shown around the world over the next few days. It convinced many travellers that airships were unsafe, and instead of balloons and bags of gas attention once again switched back to aircraft with wings.

The Wright Brothers

```
The First Real Aeroplane (US, 1903)
```

Even before Ferdinand von Zeppelin had begun building his second airship, two brothers in America were experimenting with an entirely different sort of machine, which they called the *Flyer*.

Orville and Wilbur Wright had both inherited a fascination for mechanical objects from their mother, Susan. She was keen for the boys to learn practical skills, such as carpentry. She made a wooden sledge with them, and Orville went on to make a working three-wheeled wagon. The brothers were also given mechanical toys to play with. One of their favourites was called the Flying Bat. This was made of cork and bamboo and had a small propeller that was powered by a rubber band.

As the brothers grew older they began inventing things of their own. Their worst idea was probably a new type of chewing gum made of sugar and tar (this made everyone sick), but

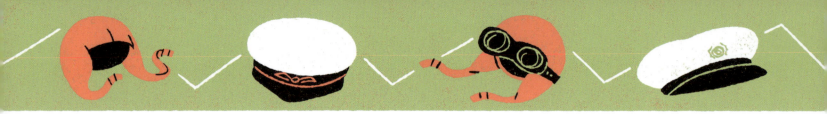

while still in their twenties they also built a full-size printing press of their own design and several bicycles. Their inventions were good enough for the brothers to set up a business selling them to customers.

The business was soon making a good profit, **but neither of the brothers forgot about the little Flying Bat** and its tightly wound rubber band. After seeing photographs of Otto Lilienthal and his gliders in the newspaper, they decided to use their woodworking skills to build a full-size mechanical flying machine.

To begin with this was just a hobby. Wilbur was convinced that it would never be possible to make money by constructing flying machines. Before building anything, they spent a lot of time reading everything they could about the new science of aeronautics. They also studied the examples of pilots like Lilienthal and the theories of a Frenchman called Octave Chanute and England's Sir George Cayley.

Cayley, in particular, had demonstrated how important it was to get the shape of the wings right. He had also explained how, by twisting the tips of the wings, it was possible to fly upwards or downwards, like a seagull. Orville and Wilbur found this very interesting, and by experimenting with large home-made kites, they managed to devise a way to twist the tips of their plane by using wires.

It was clear from Elmer of Malmesbury's mishap that air turbulence could be dangerous for any flyer. To avoid it, the pair began travelling to a remote spot called Kitty Hawk in North Carolina. The area had gentle slopes and more or less constant winds rather than sudden, violent gusts. This made it and the nearby Kill Devil Hills perfect places for the Wrights to conduct their experiments. Initially, these were made with their giant kites, but later they constructed a series of gliders using cotton cloth stretched over home-made wooden frames.

The Wrights realised that the key to success was to practise repeatedly and learn from any mistakes they made. A new design was flown like a kite on a string first, with no one on board. After this the brothers tried flying it themselves, at first from the top of a low hill, before later launches were attempted from slightly higher ones.

The brothers did everything possible to minimise the dangers faced by all early pilots. This usually meant flying only a metre or so above the ground. But even so close to earth the Wrights managed to glide hundreds of metres at a time. They also chose sandy areas for the flights as these made a soft landing much more likely.

Over the course of at least a thousand test flights **the brothers made a very important discovery**: the pilot needed to lie on his front rather than hanging down from the wings like Otto Lilienthal had done. These early gliders were very light, and by shifting his bodyweight from one side to the other, a pilot who was lying down could control the direction of flight.

After several years perfecting their glider designs, the Wrights were finally ready to add an engine. They knew they had to get exactly the right sort. In 1902 they wrote to more than a dozen different manufacturers describing the kind of engine they were looking for. It had to weigh less than 80 kilogrammes and produce at least eight or nine horsepower.

However, it didn't take long for them to discover that no one in America made a petrol engine that was suitable, so Orville and Wilbur promptly went home and built their own. This weighed only 68 kilogrammes and had even more power than they had hoped for. They had also managed to devise a clever way for a single engine to power two large wooden propellers instead of one, and by December 1903 both men felt that their new machine was ready to be put to the test at Kitty Hawk.

This machine, `the now world-famous Wright Flyer`, was larger and much heavier than any of their gliders. To help launch it they built a short wooden railway line, which they nicknamed the 'Grand Junction Railroad'. This cost less than £3 to make and was designed so that the *Flyer* could roll down it fast enough to take off.

There was still room on board for only one person, however. The brothers tossed a coin to see which of them would have the first go, and Wilbur won. On 14 December he climbed into position, but as he began to roll down the rails something went wrong and the *Flyer* tipped up and crashed into the sand.

Fortunately, the damage to the front end was only slight, but it still took a couple of days to fix. On the 17th, a freezing cold morning with a sharp wind blowing, it was Orville's turn to take the controls. The two men shook hands, and happily this time everything went according to plan. At 10.35 a.m. the *Flyer* slipped down the Grand Junction Railroad once again and then suddenly rose into the air. Only five people were there to see it happen, but the Wright brothers had achieved something incredible.

The *Flyer* didn't rise very high that day, and it didn't travel very far either, but that didn't matter. In fact, Orville was airborne for only twelve seconds and flew a mere 37 metres. That's less than the wingspan of many of today's passenger jets, but it was enough. The Wright brothers had made history: a human had flown at last, using wings and an engine.

People around the world celebrated the Wright brothers' magnificent achievement, but not everyone was happy about it. One angry member of the Aero Club in Paris said he was outraged that America had beaten France in this way. Another Frenchman bitterly refused to believe that the flight had even taken place, although there were plenty of newspaper reports about it and photographs showing Orville airborne.

But none of this carping mattered because the world's first proper aeroplane was a success and the age of powered flight had finally begun!

Louis Blériot

Crossing the English Channel
(France—England, 1909)

The truth is that the moment it became possible to do it, flying became highly competitive, and America and France weren't the only countries whose patriots and enthusiasts were racing to beat everyone else into the air. A few months after the Wrights a New Zealander called Richard Pearse managed to keep his aircraft aloft for several seconds, and in 1906 Alberto Santos-Dumont, a Brazilian, became the first person to fly an aeroplane anywhere in Europe.

Initially barely more successful than Pearse, Santos-Dumont had managed to stay up for only eight seconds on this first attempt. He won a prize from the Aero Club in Paris for flying more than a hundred metres, though, and flights soon got longer and longer as the technology improved and 'aeronauts' increased their knowledge and skills. The Wrights' third aircraft, for example, looked very much like their first one, but this time they managed to fly it more than 38 kilometres in just thirty-eight minutes. At the time a horse-drawn carriage

would have taken nearly two hours to travel the same distance.

Such achievements caused great excitement, and in 1909 the owner of the *Daily Mail* newspaper in London offered a prize of £1,000 to anyone who could successfully fly an aeroplane across the English Channel – a distance of only 32 kilometres, but with plenty of added danger.

In 1909 it was possible to buy a three-bedroom house in Britain for less than £250, so £1,000 was a huge sum of money. Four pilots immediately announced that they would be competing for the valuable prize. One was a Russian aristocrat, two were Frenchmen and the last was an Englishman called Arthur Seymour. The Wright brothers decided not to take part. They had already exceeded the 32-kilometre target but felt the prize wasn't large enough for either of them to risk his life flying over the sea.

Even now, no one is quite sure whether Seymour actually owned an aeroplane or not. He said he did, but no one ever saw it, and after entering the competition nothing more was heard from him. The Russian certainly had an aeroplane (two, in fact), and he was also known to have paid to have a few flying lessons with Wilbur Wright. After these he became the first person to fly successfully around the Eiffel Tower in Paris, but most experts still thought the most likely winner of the £1,000 prize would be one of the Frenchmen.

The first of these was an explorer and adventurer called Hubert Latham. He had already

crossed the Channel in a balloon and had made his name racing powerboats before becoming fascinated by aeroplanes. Latham's cousin owned a company which built small aircraft called Antoinettes, and Latham had asked to join the firm after watching Wilbur Wright in action. After this he had quickly learned how to take off and land, and a few weeks later managed to set a new European record by flying non-stop for an hour and seven minutes.

That was more than enough to cross the Channel, but to win the prize he would have to beat the fourth competitor, Louis Blériot, a talented inventor and engineer from northern France. Blériot's inventions included the first proper car headlights, and he spent the profits from these to design and build aircraft of his own design.

He built gliders to begin with (like Orville and Wilbur Wright had done), but then had several accidents after starting to experiment with engines. On one occasion his aircraft hit the ground nose-first and then somersaulted violently. Another time a propeller flew off, although both times Blériot somehow avoided serious injury.

Blériot wasn't really a very good pilot, but eventually his courage and patience paid off and in 1909 he finished building a delicate-looking monoplane called the *Blériot XI* (or *Blériot Eleven*). By now he had spent so much money on his dream of flying that he had run out of cash. This one, he decided, would have to do. The *XI* would have to be the machine he used to fly across the English Channel.

Blériot clearly needed the prize money more than Latham did, but Latham was better prepared and on 9 July he arrived at the French coast with his aeroplane, ready to go. More than **10,000 spectators** had gathered to see him off, and according to newspaper reports another 10,000 were waiting on the other side of the Channel, in England, to see him land. Unfortunately, wind and bad weather delayed Latham's attempt by more than a week and he was unable to take off until 19 July.

The pilot and his cousin had already demonstrated that their Antoinette could fly far enough over land to reach England, but less than halfway across the sea the engine suddenly spluttered and cut out. Latham wasn't able to restart it and was forced to land in the sea. No one had ever tried to do this before, but, remarkably, the aeroplane was undamaged and stayed afloat because it was mostly made of wood. Latham calmly lit a cigarette and waited to be rescued by the crew of a French warship that was following behind.

The Russian, Charles de Lambert, was even more unlucky. Both of his aeroplanes were badly damaged during practice flights a few kilometres along the coast. This meant it was left to Blériot to prove whether or not anyone could complete such a journey, although the unfortunate experiences of his rivals meant that even he was now beginning to wonder if he could do any better.

His wife Alice was much more optimistic, although she did know that Blériot was much better at building aircraft than at flying them. She boarded the French navy vessel that was

planning to accompany her husband's flight, and at 4.15 a.m. on 25 July Blériot finally took off in his little monoplane. Averaging 72 kph he soon overtook the warship, and for ten slightly worrying minutes he flew alone above the waves before spotting the English coastline in the distance.

Blériot didn't have a map, any instruments or even a simple compass to guide him, but as he neared the coast he saw someone on the ground waving a large red, white and blue French flag. This was the signal to begin his descent and, after circling twice, he made a bumpy landing on a grassy stretch of meadow close to the 800-year-old Dover Castle.

The monoplane's undercarriage was badly damaged by the impact, and one of the propeller blades destroyed, but once again Blériot was unhurt and he quickly climbed out. Latham was a better pilot than he was, and de Lambert was much, much richer. Each one had a more powerful engine than Blériot could afford, and a lot more flying experience, yet when it mattered most the clumsy, cash-strapped Louis had beaten them both.

Sailing across the English Channel could easily take twenty hours at this time, yet the first aeroplane to do it took just thirty-six minutes and thirty seconds. To the delight of the members of the Aero Club, both the machine and the man at the controls were French. Blériot was quickly awarded the club's special gold medal and, after being hastily repaired, his little aeroplane went on display at Selfridges department store in central London, where an incredible 150,000 people queued up to see it.

Dogfight

Aeroplanes Go into Battle (Mexico, 1913)

The first successful cross-Channel flight made people realise that aeroplanes had an exciting future ahead of them. These weren't just toys for the rich but might soon be a practical means of transport. For the first time people began to see that larger and safer aircraft could one day be used for travelling long distances very quickly instead of just buzzing around the sky and breaking records.

All this sounded exciting and positive, but it took only a very short time for more sinister uses for these machines to emerge. The Wright brothers had already been talking to senior military officers in Britain and the US about the possibility of using flying machines as weapons of war. By the end of 1909 they had sold the US Army its first aeroplane, and in Germany the government was watching the activities of Ferdinand von Zeppelin very closely.

This sort of interest can be good for inventors. Many things that we use every day are the result of wartime innovation, including waterproof coats, paper tissues, zips, stainless steel

and even wristwatches. If governments helped fund the design and construction of better aircraft, it might also make it possible for manufacturers to build them in much greater numbers.

Of course, there is a dark side to this. The technology of warfare changes all the time, but as armies become more and more mechanised, the human cost of battle nearly always seems to rise. More weapons, in other words, usually means more dead and wounded.

Fortunately, this didn't happen to begin with. In 1908 the world's first-ever military aircraft, called British Army Aeroplane No. 1, made only a few test flights before being handed back to its inventor. The one the Wright brothers sold to the US Army a year later was similarly used for training, not fighting. Neither of them had room for guns or bombs, and neither was ever used in battle.

It wasn't until 1913 that airmen first fought each other in mid-air. This occurred during the Mexican Revolution in Central America, when two American pilots, fighting on opposite sides, began firing pistols at each other in what became known as a dogfight. Fortunately, no one was killed or even injured, and one of the Americans later explained why this was. He said he had deliberately aimed to miss because he didn't want to hurt the other pilot. The two were old friends, even though they found themselves on opposing sides of the revolution.

Even during World War I (1914–18) aircraft were mostly used for spying on the enemy to begin with. A pilot flying high above a battlefield was well placed to observe the enemy on the ground below. He could warn soldiers on his own side if they were about to be attacked and use a camera to take photographs of woods and other areas where enemy troops had hidden their big guns.

This sort of reconnaissance work was highly dangerous, however, because no one likes being spied on and aircraft built of wood and canvas were incredibly fragile. Because these early machines were also unarmed the only way for an airman to stay out of trouble was usually to fly away as fast as possible. At least one British pilot had to do this with his finger pressed against a hole in his engine's fuel tank after it was punctured by a lucky long-distance shot from a German soldier.

In many cases a single bullet fired from a rifle would be enough to cause an aeroplane to crash into the ground, although one flyer somehow survived after more than 600 explosive artillery rounds were fired at him during a forty-minute flight over a battlefield in northern France.

Pilots were naturally horrified by incidents like this and slowly began to devise their own ways of staying safe and fighting back. Some of their ideas were slightly bizarre, such as throwing bricks at each other or dropping a length of rope on to an enemy aircraft below in the hope that it would get tangled up in the propeller. One Russian was killed after deliberately

43

ramming his own aeroplane into one flown by an enemy pilot.

To begin with only one aeroplane in the whole of the British Royal Flying Corps had a machine gun. This had been fitted to it (unofficially) at the request of the pilot, and it wasn't until manufacturers began installing weapons in their own aircraft that **the era of air combat really began**. There were plenty of problems even then. Pilots sometimes shot their own propellers off by mistake during dogfights, and aircraft were often attacked by their own side because they all looked quite similar to the soldiers on the ground.

World War I aircraft were also very basic, and without any sophisticated navigational aids to help them, pilots occasionally had to land in a field to ask a farmer for directions. Another of their tricks was to fly low enough to read the names of railway stations and other local landmarks, or to keep an old road map on the floor of the cockpit. Needless to say, all three methods of navigation could be highly dangerous.

Perhaps because of this it took several years for the most senior military planners to fully understand how useful aircraft could be. At the start of the war many of them didn't really trust new technology of any sort, and some needed a lot of persuading. By the end, however, a staggering 200,000 or more aircraft had seen action in Europe and the Middle East. Most of these were fighters that fought each other in the skies above the battlefield. Other, much larger ones called bombers (together with several German airships) were used to drop thousands of tonnes of high explosives on troops and on towns and cities.

The results of this were terrible: on 13 June 1917, in a single German raid on London, 162 people were killed and more than 400 injured. But increased government funding and the demands of the military also had a very positive impact on aviation. Aeroplanes of all types were growing larger, faster, more powerful and far more reliable. By 1918 they were better in every way than anything even Louis Blériot or Wilbur and Orville Wright could have imagined at the start of the conflict, just four years earlier.

The end of the war brought another benefit too, when hundreds of unwanted bombers were sold off to the public for as little as £40 each. Many were quickly converted into the first proper passenger planes, and having learned to fly as servicemen, there were now plenty of pilots available to begin flying them for a living.

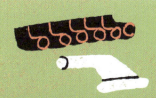

Katherine Stinson

Looping the Loop in a Flying Circus (US, 1915)

While military pilots were battling each other in the skies over Europe and the Middle East, many American pilots were using aeroplanes for fun and making lots of money at the same time.

With rival manufacturers producing more and more aircraft, public air displays had become hugely popular. Flying daredevils known as barnstormers had begun travelling around the US to show people what these exciting new machines could do.

To begin with the barnstormers were all men, and a typical air display would involve them performing a variety of tricks and stunts in front of huge crowds of excited spectators. These sometimes included wing-walking, whereby an individual would climb out of the cockpit and on to the wing. A few would even clamber from one aeroplane to another while flying high above the spectators.

At a time when most people had never even been in a car, thousands of people paid to watch the biggest shows, which were known as flying circuses. Pilots would fly low over small cities and country towns to publicise these events, performing high-speed dives and spins before landing in a suitable field. The most famous pilots became national celebrities, and one of them, an enthusiastic showman called Lincoln Beachey, is estimated to have entertained 17 million spectators in a single year.

Beachey's aerobatic feats included racing against express trains and flying figure-of-eights, but he also liked breaking records. On one occasion `he flew in an upwards spiral for more than an hour and a half`. By the time his fuel ran out, at more than 3,500 metres, he was frozen stiff, but he put his aircraft into a steep dive and glided safely back down to the ground. Even more incredibly, Beachey became the first pilot to fly around *inside* a building, reaching a speed of 100 kph at the Machinery Palace in San Francisco.

For a long time these barnstormers insisted that their exploits were far too dangerous for any women to join in. Aircraft engines, they said, were too noisy, filthy and unreliable. The wooden frames they were attached to sometimes broke and occasionally wings actually snapped right off. The men were completely exposed to the wind and bad weather, and every year a number of them were killed or seriously injured when stunts went wrong.

The Wright brothers had opened America's first flying school in 1910, and despite the dangers, others soon began operating up and down the country. Learning to fly was expensive, but many of these schools simply refused to teach female students, even if they had enough money. You had to be an especially determined young woman to overcome this prejudice, and one of the very first to do so was an adventurous teenager called Katherine Stinson.

Stinson had learned to drive her father's Ford Model T when she was only fourteen. Not long afterwards she was offered a ride in a balloon, and it completely changed her life. Before she went up in the air she had dreamed of becoming a professional pianist, but by the time she came down all she could think about was selling her piano to pay for flying lessons.

Annoyingly, because she was a woman, her first instructor would only allow her to sit and watch him operating the controls. For the same reason, the second wouldn't even let her climb into his aeroplane. Fortunately, when she managed to change his mind, he quickly realised that she had a natural talent for flying an aircraft. Because of this she was allowed to make her first solo flight after just four hours of instruction.

From now on all Stinson wanted to do was to fly. So far, only three other American women had qualified for a pilot's licence, but as soon as Stinson received hers she started saving up to buy an aeroplane of her own. The newspapers immediately nicknamed her 'the flying schoolgirl', although she was a first-class mechanic as well as a good pilot. She serviced her own engine, and when something on her aircraft broke she usually knew how to fix it herself.

By 1913 she had made history by becoming the first female pilot to be authorised by the US government to carry bags of mail by air. Stinson was also the first woman to fly an aeroplane in China and Japan, possibly the first to fly anywhere in the dark, and the first American (male or female) to fly more than 600 miles (or nearly 1,000 kilometres) without stopping to rest or refuel.

With her sister Marjorie she also became the first woman in the world to own and run a flying school. The pair trained dozens of military pilots during World War I, but when the army turned down Stinson's own application to join up and fight (again, because she was a woman) she began to organise flying displays in her Curtiss biplane, which raised nearly $2 million to help the Red Cross treat the wounded.

Clearly, Stinson took anything to do with aviation very seriously, but she wanted to have fun with it as well. Besides breaking records and making history, she soon became famous across America for her stunt-flying in various different aeroplanes. It must have helped that once the barnstormers had finally been persuaded that females could fly after all, they quickly discovered just how much the public loved seeing women doing it.

Stinson certainly enjoyed all the attention she got, and she delighted spectators by decorating her aeroplane with roses before leading a new year parade of aircraft above the streets of Pasadena. She is also believed to have invented the art of skywriting by fixing burning flares to her wings and then using them to spell out 'C A L' in gigantic glowing letters across the night sky over California.

The trick everyone loved best, however, was looping the loop. This is a highly dangerous manoeuvre that involves flying an aeroplane in a huge vertical circle. For much of the time both the aeroplane and the pilot are upside down, and most Americans had never seen anyone do it before Stinson completed her first loop in 1915.

In a fragile aeroplane with an open cockpit there is a genuine risk that a pilot might fall out while performing the stunt. Aircraft and pilots are subjected to enormous stresses during this sort of high-speed manoeuvre. What scientists call G-forces can do severe damage to a looping aircraft and cause the pilot to lose control after blacking out or fainting.

None of this seemed to worry Stinson, however. After doing her first loop she went straight back up to try again. Before long she had invented her own, even more dangerous version, which combined a loop with a roll at the very top. She called this the Dippy Twist Loop, and it caused a sensation, just as she hoped it would.

Sadly, Stinson had to retire from flying when she was only about thirty after falling ill with a disease called tuberculosis. Despite this, she made a new career for herself as an award-winning architect, and she is still regarded as one of the greatest pilots of the pioneering era.

Queen Bess

The First Black Woman Pilot (France, 1921)

Bessie Coleman had an even shorter flying career than Katherine Stinson but is perhaps even more famous thanks to her being the first black person in the world to qualify for an international pilot's licence.

Coleman was born in Texas and had twelve brothers and sisters. Her mother was African American and her father was of Native American descent, a member of the indigenous Cherokee people. They were poor farmers, and the entire family lived in a cabin with only one room. Neither parent could read or write, but their daughter Bessie did well enough at school to win a place at university, although she dropped out before finishing her degree.

Coleman got a job in a barber's shop in the city of Chicago, where she became fascinated by the stories she heard about American pilots in Europe during World War I. She was determined to learn to fly, although she knew this would be extremely difficult for someone like her. Having been through an educational system that was segregated, meaning black

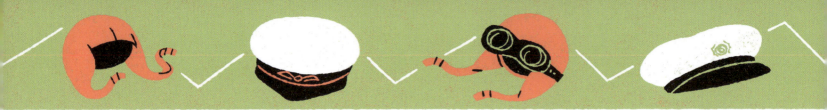

and white children were taught separately, Coleman, like Stinson, found that nearly all the flying schools in America would teach only white men.

One option was to move abroad, as she had heard that French women were allowed to fly aeroplanes on their own. Coleman began learning to speak French after meeting two successful African American businessmen who said they would pay for her to go. In 1920, aged twenty-eight, Coleman boarded a ship to France. Once there she found a flying school on the coast about 200 km from Paris, and the owners agreed to teach her how to fly.

The young woman had never flown before, not even in a balloon, but she was an excellent student and found her first experience in a Nieuport two-seater totally exhilarating. A few weeks later she was badly shaken up after seeing another student die when his identical aeroplane crashed, but she refused to give up. If anything, the shock of the accident made her even more determined to succeed, and in 1921 Coleman was finally **awarded her international pilot's licence**.

She went back home to the US, where several new companies were beginning to fly fare-paying passengers around the country. Unfortunately, Coleman knew that no airline would employ a black person as a pilot. She needed to earn a living, however, and thought that people might pay to see and hear the only black female pilot in America. She was right about this, and before long she was travelling around making speeches about her adventures and showing black-and-white films of her time in France.

Coleman bravely refused to do talks to segregated audiences and said she wouldn't lecture in places that discriminated against African Americans. Despite this, she received many invitations to speak, and the large audiences she attracted helped her earn enough money to start flying again.

The plan now was to become a barnstormer or display pilot. The public still wasn't used to the idea of women flying aeroplanes, and `no one in America had ever seen a black or Native American woman do it before`. Several newspapers sent reporters to interview her, and as her inspiring story became more widely known her daring flying displays began to attract enormous crowds. Coleman performed many of the same high-speed stunts and manoeuvres as Stinson, including looping the loop and flying figure-of-eights. However, she also did some wing-walking and taught herself how to use a parachute.

Spectators found this just as thrilling because parachutes were still quite a new idea. The technology was highly experimental, and one inventor had already been killed when testing his own design by leaping off the Eiffel Tower in Paris. The horror of this tragedy just added to the sense of excitement, though, and watching a person deliberately jump out of an aeroplane must have provided exactly the sort of heart-stopping moments that display organisers needed to thrill the public.

Coleman had been barnstorming for about two years before she had her first big accident,

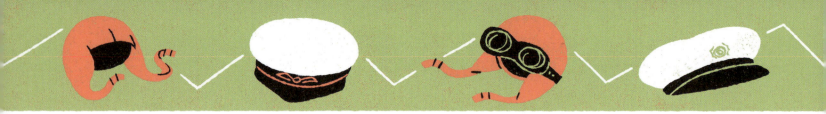

when her engine suddenly coughed and died and her aeroplane ploughed into the ground. The machine was completely destroyed, while she was badly injured by the impact and left with a broken leg, several cracked ribs and numerous cuts and bruises.

It took several months for her to recover, and it was nearly two years before she could afford to buy another aeroplane to replace the one that had been wrecked. When she returned to the air she found that she was more popular than ever. Spectators called her 'Queen Bess' or 'Brave Bess' and flocked to see her displays in even greater numbers.

By now, as well as doing displays, Coleman had started teaching others to fly. She did everything she could to encourage other women – and especially African American women – to follow her example. She also continued `the fight against the terrible discrimination` and segregation that she had suffered herself.

A good example of this came in 1925, when she flew back to her home state of Texas to put on a display there. She refused to take part after learning that all the African American and Native American spectators were expected to use different gates to the white ones. She had several meetings with the organisers, who couldn't ignore her as she was one of the most popular barnstormers in the whole country. Eventually they agreed that everyone could use the same gates but that black and white spectators would still have to stand in different areas to watch the show.

Coleman didn't like this idea much either but she reluctantly agreed to put on a show anyway. She may have decided that it would be a good thing for ordinary white people to see a black woman doing something extraordinary. Others certainly thought so, and many of them applauded her for standing up for her beliefs even after she had become a celebrity.

Coleman herself always believed that the best way to demonstrate that black people can do the same jobs as white people is for them to actually do those jobs. For this reason she wanted to open the first-ever African American flying school in order to train more black pilots, but unfortunately tragedy stuck before she was able to do this.

It happened in April 1926, when Coleman, who was still only thirty-four years old, was flying in Florida with another pilot called William Wills. One of his tools had been left in the cockpit and it became wedged in the controls of the aircraft. This meant Wills couldn't fly it properly, and the pair suddenly found themselves flipping upside down. Coleman wasn't wearing a seatbelt (or a parachute) and she fell out of the aircraft, before plummeting nearly a thousand metres down to the ground.

Queen Bess didn't stand a chance. She was killed instantly, and Wills died seconds later when his aeroplane crashed a couple of metres away from her body. People were naturally shocked by this double disaster and they could hardly believe that such a well-known and talented pilot had died while flying as a passenger. It was a terrible end, even by barnstorming standards, but what an extraordinary life.

Alan Cobham

To Australia and Back Again (1926)

While Bessie Coleman was delighting crowds of onlookers in the US, an adventurous young Englishman called Alan Cobham was clocking up longer and longer flights around Europe and Asia and across the African continent.

Cobham had trained as a pilot in the Royal Flying Corps during World War I and became hooked on flying. At the end of the war he bought an ex-military Avro two-seater with a couple of friends. The men took members of the public on what they called 'five-bob flips' – charging them 25p for a short flight in the Avro – but then Cobham found a much better job as a test pilot for the newly formed de Havilland Aircraft Company.

The company's owner recognised the huge publicity value of adventurous pilots like Cobham and their record-breaking flights. If he could demonstrate that de Havilland aircraft flew faster and over

longer distances than those of his rivals, it would be the best possible advertisement for the machines made in his factory.

Cobham was happy to help, and in 1921 he took off from an airstrip near London in one of de Havilland's aircraft for a tiring tour of seventeen European cities. He flew a **record-breaking 8,000 kilometres in just three weeks**, and as soon as the company launched its new DH50 model, Cobham took to the air again to win several prizes by demonstrating its speed and reliability. The awards included one for flying from Copenhagen in Denmark to the Swedish city of Gothenburg, and another for his performance in the prestigious King's Cup race. This is a British long-distance cross-country race, and Cobham won it at his first attempt after flying the equivalent of eight times around the M25 motorway. He did this at an average speed of more than 160 kph.

Cobham was addicted to flying, and so the following year he set off in a second DH50 to fly even further – from Surrey all the way to South Africa. The journey, from Croydon to Cape Town and back again, was an exhausting 25,000 kilometres, but by the time Cobham had completed the flight he was already planning something even more spectacular.

This time Cobham told his boss at de Havilland that he was going to fly from Kent to London – via Australia! Before setting off on this epic journey, he ordered a pair of large floats to be fitted to the DH50 so it could take off and land on water. Cobham had never tried this

before, but in countries where there weren't any airports or runways the floats would enable him to land on a river or even a large lake.

Cobham's trusted engineer Arthur Elliot came along as his companion on this flight. The pair had already flown together on several long-distance journeys, and Cobham always said it was Elliot's skill as a mechanic which ensured that his engines ran for hundreds of hours without any serious problems.

Even so, the two men knew there would be many dangers ahead of them besides the normal hazards associated with flying. A revolver and a rifle were put on board in case they had to land in hostile territory or came down in the wild, where it might be necessary to shoot their own dinner. Also, Elliot didn't have any experience of trying to fix an aircraft as it bobbed around on the water. If he dropped a tool while working or an essential piece of equipment, it would be lost for ever beneath the waves.

The two refused to be put off, however, and they left England in June 1926, after just three or four practice runs at taking off and landing on the River Medway in Kent. It must have seemed incredible to everyone watching them take off that they were bound for the other side of the world.

During the early stages of the journey they made some very long flights between refuelling stops. The DH50 successfully crossed the whole of France

non-stop. The next stage took them several hundred kilometres over the sea and they landed in Italy as darkness fell.

After flying through Greece and Turkey they reached the Middle East, but then disaster struck. In Iraq the aircraft was forced down by a ferocious dust storm, and Cobham struggled to find anywhere he could land in the swampy, overgrown landscape. Eventually he found a safe place and was busy congratulating himself on a successful landing when the aircraft was shaken by a loud bang. He shouted to Elliot, who was sitting behind him. The mechanic said there was fuel leaking from a burst pipe and that his arm was bleeding really heavily. When Cobham turned around and saw how pale his friend's face was he realised that Elliot had been seriously injured in the explosion.

Cobham couldn't decide whether to try some basic first aid on him or to fly as quickly as possible to the nearest hospital. This was at least 150 kilometres away, but Cobham thought it would give Elliot the best possible chance of survival. Getting there involved flying very low over unfamiliar territory and in conditions of extremely poor visibility. Despite these difficulties he made it in under forty minutes, but Elliot was now even weaker and very sadly died the next day.

Cobham was extremely shocked by the loss of his friend, especially when he discovered a hole in the aircraft's side. It turned out they had been shot at by an Iraqi villager, possibly one who had been terrified by the sight of the first aeroplane he'd ever seen

suddenly appearing out of the dust storm. The bullet had passed through the aircraft's body and injured Elliot fatally.

For a while it looked like the journey was over, but Cobham was determined to press on, so the Royal Air Force (RAF) offered to send him a new mechanic, Sergeant Ward. The aircraft was carefully patched up, and the two men continued the long journey through India and Burma to Singapore and the islands of the Dutch East Indies.

Cobham averaged an impressive `800 kilometres a day`, including one exceptionally long and dangerous flight across a wide stretch of open water. The little DH50 was repeatedly battered by strong headwinds and heavy monsoon rains, and Cobham often had to wrestle with the controls just to stay on course. For much of the final stage of the journey the aircraft's wings were just a few metres above the dangerous currents of the Indian Ocean, but just when the exhausted pair were beginning to lose hope, one of them finally spotted their destination. Their relief must have been enormous, and on 5 August they made the perfect safe landing in Australia.

Cobham decided he wanted to spend some time flying around Australia before flying back to England, but after this the return flight went without a hitch. He and Ward reached England in October and were greeted by the sight of thousands of cheering Londoners on Westminster Bridge. Always happy to put on a show, Cobham flew low over the Houses of Parliament and then circled round before splashing down on the River Thames.

Over the course of three months the DH50 had spent 320 hours in the air and covered an astonishing 45,000 kilometres. It was the best possible result for the de Havilland Aircraft Company and a magnificent achievement on the part of its pilot and his two mechanics. The great globetrotter was knighted shortly afterwards by a delighted King George V. Today Sir Alan Cobham is recognised as an important pioneer of long-distance flying and the man who helped pave the way for the modern era of international aviation.

Charles Lindbergh

Alone Above the Atlantic (Atlantic Ocean, 1927)

In 1919 two British aviators, John Alcock and Arthur Brown, had flown through ferocious Atlantic storms to win another generous *Daily Mail* prize, this time worth £10,000. No one had flown non-stop across the Atlantic before them, and no one managed to do it again until eight years later, after an American announced that he was going to do it all on his own.

Charles Lindbergh had worked as a barnstormer and an airmail pilot, so he already understood the dangers of flying. However, in the 1920s even the most experienced long-distance pilots still preferred to fly as close to the coastline as possible. Doing this made navigation much easier, and it was much safer at a time when aircraft engines still weren't very reliable. Lindbergh knew this perfectly well, but staying close to the coastline wasn't an option for anyone trying to cross one of the world's great oceans.

The distances involved in trans-oceanic flights are so huge that a pilot could go for days, not just hours, without even seeing dry land. Alcock and Brown had flown a total of 3,630 kilometres over the waves to get from Canada to Clifden in Ireland. Now Lindbergh was planning to fly even further: 5,800 kilometres from an airfield in New York to one in Paris.

Plenty of people had already tried this and failed. A French pilot was badly injured when his aircraft burst into flames on take-off, and two more disappeared and were never seen again. They probably crashed in a storm, although for years there was a rumour that their aeroplane had been shot down by smugglers. An American pilot also crashed during his attempt. He was lucky and escaped injury, but just days afterwards two more were killed during their final test flight.

Most of these attempts had been very expensive to organise, but Lindbergh knew he had only $2,000 to spend. As an airmail pilot he was used to flying long distances on his own, although once he had to parachute to safety after accidentally running out of fuel. He had a theory that the earlier attempts had failed because the aircraft used were too large and too heavy. To avoid making the same mistake he asked a manufacturer called Ryan Airlines to build him a much smaller, much lighter machine.

Incredibly, the aircraft was ready to fly just two months later. Lindbergh called it the *Spirit of St Louis* after some rich businessmen in the city of St Louis agreed to pay Ryan's bill. The new machine had only one engine because Lindbergh believed that more engines simply meant there was more to go wrong. He had also asked for a silver body that was sleek and streamlined so he could fly as far as possible without using too much fuel.

It still needed five fuel tanks, however, including two huge ones located in front of the cramped, dark cockpit. This meant Lindbergh wouldn't be able to see where he was going or stretch his legs. His only view out would be through the small windows on either side of his seat. To read the compass, which was positioned behind him, he would have to use a tiny mirror from a make-up case. This had been stuck to the ceiling of the aeroplane with a piece of chewing gum.

Radio and newspaper reports on the deaths and disappearances of his rivals had increased the public's interest in the transatlantic adventure enormously. Lindbergh, as the latest contender, had to fly more than 4,000 kilometres from California just to reach the starting point in New York. By the time he arrived an excited crowd was there to see him off, but unfortunately bad weather delayed his departure.

When he finally took off in drizzly rain on 20 May few onlookers thought he had much chance of success in such a small, funny-looking aeroplane. Lindbergh also realised, to his horror, that he was already feeling a bit sleepy. This was almost certainly a result of his long journey from California, and for the rest of the flight staying awake turned out to be one of the greatest challenges the lone pilot faced.

Once Lindbergh was out over the ocean it wasn't long before he ran into the same kind of thick fog banks, snow and sleet that had troubled Alcock and Brown. In the freezing air the cabin of the *Spirit of St Louis* got colder and colder and worrying amounts of ice began to form on the wings and body. This can be fatal as ice increases an aircraft's weight and makes it much harder to control. The exhausted pilot also found that sticking his head out of the window into the freezing-cold air was the only way he could be sure to stay awake.

Lindbergh still found himself daydreaming despite the cold, and occasionally he even dropped off to sleep. Whenever he did, the aeroplane would begin to suddenly dive downwards, and Lindbergh would be jerked awake by the worrying change in engine noise. It must have been even harder staying conscious once darkness began to fall, but the following morning the *Spirit of St Louis* was still in the air. Hours later Lindbergh could tell he was nearing land again when he saw fishing boats and soaring seagulls beneath him, and at 10.22 p.m. on the second day he finally touched down in Paris.

After thirty-three and a half hours alone in the air, it must have been a shock to be suddenly surrounded by 150,000 noisy well-wishers. Lindbergh was carried aloft by excited spectators for nearly an hour, and the wild celebrations were spoiled only by Parisian souvenir-hunters tearing bits off what had now become the most famous flying machine in the world.

This time no one seemed to mind much that Europe had been beaten by America again, and when Lindbergh flew over to London he received an even bigger, even warmer welcome than in Paris. Both sides of the runway at Croydon Aerodrome were thronged with thousands of people, and when the aircraft rolled to a halt the crowd around it was so huge that Lindbergh couldn't be seen.

America, understandably, went wilder still, and once Lindbergh had travelled back by sea similar celebrations were soon repeated in every town or city that he visited. Around the world everyone wanted to meet aviation's newest hero and shake his hand: not just the press and the public but Hollywood stars and even royalty.

Lindbergh had always been a very private man and he found all this attention very uncomfortable. When his baby son was killed during a bungled kidnap attempt (by a criminal hoping to cash in on the father's fame) Lindbergh's life fell apart. He and his wife Anne left America for Europe and rented a home in the quiet English countryside.

The Lindberghs only returned to the US a few years later, and Charles went on to make a number of political speeches in the months before World War II (1939–45). Many of the views he expressed in these were deeply racist, and he spoke of his admiration for Adolf Hitler and his murderous regime in Germany. Many Americans, including President Franklin D. Roosevelt, were horrified by this and became convinced that Lindbergh was a Nazi.

Unsurprisingly, Lindbergh's reputation has never recovered from this. His skill and courage as a flyer has never been in any doubt, however, and the *Spirit of St Louis* has long been one of the most popular exhibits on display at the Smithsonian Institution in Washington.

Seaplanes

The Need for Speed (Italy, 1927)

International aircraft manufacturers were always interested in speed as well as endurance. Charles Lindbergh's *Spirit of St Louis* had a top speed of 210 kph, at a time when most cars could manage only 70 or 80. However, bigger engines and improved wing designs meant that specialised racing aircraft were soon beginning to offer even better performance.

A French aviation enthusiast called Jacques Schneider was particularly interested in improving aerodynamics and engine design. In 1913 he began organising races to encourage manufacturers around the world to build better, faster aircraft. These had to be able to take off and land on water.

Schneider paid for a lavish bronze and solid silver trophy, which a national team could keep if it won three races within a five-year period. This idea appealed strongly to the patriotism of many pilots from Britain, France, Italy, Switzerland and the US. The public loved the idea

too. The races were run over a triangular course of between 280 and 350 kilometres and attracted hundreds of thousands of spectators. They moved from nation to nation because the winning team got to hold the next event in its own country.

The quality of the competition varied widely from year to year. In 1924, for example, only the US entered because no one else had any suitable aircraft ready. After flying alone around the course at a leisurely pace the Americans sportingly declared that their win didn't count. However, the competition was usually intense as the world's finest pilots – sitting at the controls of what at this time were the fastest machines on Earth – raced around the triangular course in a breathtaking demonstration of stamina, skill and courage.

Every country wanted to win, and by pitting Italians against Americans, and Frenchmen against Englishmen, the races did a great deal to improve aircraft design – just as Schneider had hoped. By 1926 the best aeroplanes were nearly twice as fast as the *Spirit of St Louis* and four of the five countries had won at least one race.

The Italians appeared most likely to win the 1927 race but no one had managed to win three times out of five, so the wonderful trophy was still up for grabs. Britain's last win had been with a clumsy-looking biplane called the Sea Lion. It was embarrassingly old-fashioned compared to Italy's Macchi Castoldi and the American Curtiss, so when its replacement crashed, the Supermarine company decided to build an entirely new, much sleeker design, which it called the S5.

Reginald Mitchell created something both beautiful and highly aerodynamic. The body was made of a lightweight metal called duralumin, with slender wings and copper radiators to cool the plane's enormous twelve-cylinder engine. This produced around 900 horsepower, making it more than four times as powerful as the engine that had taken Lindbergh from one side of the Atlantic to the other.

Two S5s took part in the 1927 race at Venice in Italy, and both performed brilliantly. Britain came first and second, and the winner, an RAF pilot called Sidney Webster, managed to average `more than 450 kph`. This was a fantastic result, although tragedy struck shortly afterwards when the pilot of a third S5 was killed while attempting to set a new speed world record.

Partly because of this, Mitchell introduced numerous modifications for the next race, which was held two years later in southern England. The S6 looked like its predecessor but had an entirely new engine, the mammoth Rolls-Royce R. This also had twelve cylinders but produced an additional 1,000 horsepower. It was the brainchild of Sir Henry Royce, who had used his walking stick to trace out the basic design for it in the sand of a beach in Sussex.

Sir Henry is still regarded as one of Britain's most talented engineers, and this new V12 engine eventually went on to break all the speed world records for cars, boats and aircraft – something that no other engine has ever managed to do. Perhaps unsurprisingly the R also

turned out to be a race winner, powering Mitchell's sleek S6 to victory in the 1929 event, at an average speed of almost 530 kph.

If Britain could win a third race in 1931, it could keep the trophy, but at this critical moment Supermarine ran out of money. Things were looking desperate, until a famous women's rights campaigner called Lucy Houston offered the company £100,000 of her own money. Fortunately, her extraordinary donation encouraged the government to step in, and with only nine months to go race fans began to hear thrilling rumours of yet another spectacular new aeroplane called the Supermarine S6B.

Mitchell had been hard at work making small but important adjustments to his earlier design so that it could accommodate an even faster, even more powerful version of the Rolls-Royce R. This used a special blend of fuel and a device called a supercharger to produce **an astonishing 2,350 horsepower**. None of the other teams had anything to match it, and in September 1931 Supermarine won the race yet again when the RAF's Flight Lieutenant John Boothman lapped the circuit at nearly 550 kph. The stresses needed to do this were reportedly so great that the S6B's engine needed to be completely rebuilt after less than an hour in the air. However, the third win meant Britain got to keep the precious trophy, and amid great celebrations the winning aircraft was put on permanent display at the Science Museum in London.

Nearly a hundred years later Supermarine is still one of the best-known names in aviation.

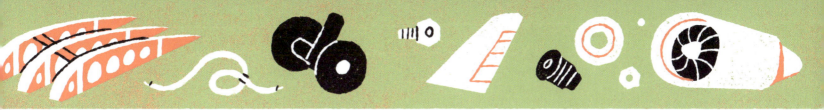

This isn't just because Mitchell's spectacular machines won more races; without the S6 and S6B the world-famous Spitfire would never have existed and Britain could well have lost World War II. The Spitfire's design, another of Mitchell's, was based very closely on his earlier seaplanes, and its high-performance Merlin engine was developed from the same remarkable R-type that Sir Henry Royce had first sketched out in the sand with his stick.

Jacques Schneider could not have wished for a better legacy than the Spitfire. He always hoped his race series would thrill spectators and that the competitive spirit of the teams would dramatically improve aircraft quality and performance – and that's exactly what happened. He didn't live long enough to witness the triple triumph of Mitchell's magnificent monoplanes, nor indeed the defeat of Hitler's Germany (sadly, he died in 1928), but `his legacy is clear to all`. The Schneider Trophy races brilliantly achieved their creator's aims and then, years later, they helped to change the course of history.

The TsAGI 1-EA

The First Helicopter Lifts Off (Russia, 1932)

While some countries were proud to show off their latest aircraft in competitions and at public events, others preferred to work away in secret.

The Russians certainly did, which is one of the reasons why, even now, so little is known about the mysterious and oddly named TsAGI 1-EA. This was nowhere near as fast as the Supermarine S6, and it couldn't fly very far either, unlike the *Spirit of St Louis*. But what it could do was take off and land vertically, which meant that like modern helicopters it didn't need a long runway or even a smooth stretch of water.

The TsAGI organisation was established in Russia more than a hundred years ago, but it still carries out important research into new aircraft design and even space travel. Its technicians and engineers have been the brains behind numerous airliners, fighter jets and spacecraft, as well as building one of the world's first working helicopters. They called this the 1-EA, meaning 'Experimental Apparatus No. 1'.

Helicopters had already been around for centuries, but only as an idea. At least 2,000 years ago the Chinese were making a children's toy called a top, which had a small propeller on top of a bamboo stick. Spinning the stick made the propeller rotate so the toy could take off and fly for a few seconds. About 1,500 years later the Italian inventor Leonardo da Vinci drew up detailed plans for a much larger, spiral-shaped machine. It would have been large enough to lift a person off the ground, except that no country at this time had the technology needed to make it work.

However, interest in the idea never went away. This is probably because people like da Vinci realised that a machine that could take off and land vertically would have many different uses.

Today helicopters make it possible to fly passengers right into the heart of a city, before landing on the flat roof of a tall building or even in the street. They have also taken part in hundreds of humanitarian missions, dropping medical supplies into disaster zones or flying food and water into regions affected by famine and drought. Air ambulances have similarly saved thousands of lives in Britain alone, and search-and-rescue operations (at sea and on land) would be much harder and more dangerous without helicopters.

Helicopters are also useful to the military, for flying troops and equipment to places where aeroplanes can't land, although it took many years before the complex technology needed to make them fly properly was fully understood. In order to take to the air a helicopter needs

a rotor, which is a sort of large propeller with blades that face upwards instead of forwards. When the blades spin round at high speed each one acts a bit like the wing of an aeroplane, except that an aeroplane has to keep moving forward to stay airborne and a helicopter doesn't. An aeroplane needs to do this to keep air passing over the wings or it will lose lift. A helicopter doesn't because the lift is generated by its blades moving through the air as they spin. This also means a pilot can `fly forwards, backwards and even sideways` just by tilting the rotor blades in the right direction. Helicopters can fly straight up and down too, but just as importantly, the pilot can stay in one position for long periods. This ability to hover helps explain why helicopters are so useful for the sorts of tasks listed above.

In the 1930s inventors in several different countries were trying to build prototype helicopters that actually worked. One of them was a Russian scientist called Alexei Cheremukhin. He had been an army pilot during World War I, before getting a job at TsAGI, where he helped design a small airliner that successfully flew more than 7,000 kilometres around Russia and China.

His design for a helicopter looks extremely basic now, but when he produced the first detailed drawings of it in 1928 they were much better than rival ideas by others at TsAGI. Because of this, Cheremukhin was given permission to build a working prototype. When it was finished, the prototype had no bodywork, just a web of steel tubes welded together to

form something that looked a bit like a climbing frame. It had two petrol engines and small spinning rotors at either end. The large, main, four-bladed rotor was mounted on top of the frame, above the engines and just behind the pilot.

In the same way that the Wright brothers tested their early machines by flying them like kites, the first flight of the 1-EA was made in 1930 with it tethered to the ground using cables. Cheremukhin wanted to fly it himself, and the cables were intended to prevent it flying too high if he lost control. They would also lessen the damage to both pilot and prototype if he crashed.

Happily, this didn't happen, and by August 1932 Cheremukhin felt confident enough to fly the 1-EA without any cables. On 1 August he took it to a height of 160 metres and managed to fly for around for twelve minutes. Two weeks later he reached 605 metres and stayed up even longer. This was `more than thirty times higher` than any other prototype had managed so far, but it was never officially recognised as a new world record. This was because the secretive communist Soviet government refused to let Cheremukhin talk about his achievement, even in his own country. They were determined not to let foreign countries find out what he had done, so although Cheremukhin was promoted and became a professor, the 1-EA was still considered top secret when it was destroyed in a crash two years later. Even after this, it was several decades before aviation enthusiasts outside Russia found out what its inventor had been up to.

Douglas Douglas-Hamilton

A Daring Flight Over Everest (Nepal, 1933)

In the 1930s no one had managed to climb to the top of the world's highest mountain, Everest in Nepal. Several teams of experienced mountaineers had attempted to reach the 8,848-metre summit but failed, and nearly a dozen climbers had died trying.

In 1933 a British team decided to do something completely different. The millionairess Lucy Houston, who had already donated £100,000 to help Britain win the Schneider Trophy air race, now offered even more money to pay for an expedition to Asia's vast Himalayan mountain range, where the RAF would attempt to fly over the top of its highest peak.

Many mountaineers thought this was cheating and wouldn't count as reaching the summit. However, Squadron Leader Douglas Douglas-Hamilton actually had no plans to land on top of Everest. He was more interested in proving that an aircraft could fly over it, and he wanted to take along a passenger to photograph the ice and thick snow covering the mountain's upper slopes. His plan was for these highly detailed black-and-white images to be used to identify new routes for future British expeditions to tackle the mountain on foot.

Flying to a very high altitude was easier than mountain climbing, but the dangers were enormous even for an experienced pilot like Douglas-Hamilton. His aircraft was a Westland PV-3, a biplane built to attack warships by dropping a large torpedo into the sea. However, it still had an open cockpit and a nine-cylinder engine based on a plane designed many years previously during World War I.

Scientists already knew that air gets thinner and thinner the higher you go. At 8,000 metres it contains only around a third of the oxygen that most humans are used to. This makes it very difficult to breathe, which is why mountaineers call the slopes above this height 'the death zone'. It's also a lot colder than at sea level, making it yet more dangerous.

Even the smaller peaks in the Himalayas are higher than most mountains anywhere else in the world. The temperature there often plunges to 40 degrees Celsius below zero or worse, and the winds on Everest itself are ferocious. These can blow at 275 kph in all directions, and yet pilots at this time, like mountaineers, had none of the protective clothing that exists today. Most wore only warm leather boots and multiple layers of ordinary wool and cotton fabric, although special sheepskin flying suits were ordered for this particular flight.

When the idea of flying over Everest was first suggested, many professional pilots just didn't think it was possible. Admiral Mark Kerr, one of the founders of the RAF, said he thought it would be at least a hundred years before aeroplanes were able to fly high enough to do so. Cockpits could be fitted with heaters and oxygen tanks to help pilots cope with the cold, thin atmosphere, but propellers don't work at all well in such air. In the 1930s neither did most aircraft engines, because they needed oxygen as well as fuel to function effectively.

The team were sure they could do it, however. A second Westland aircraft was selected to accompany the squadron leader, and both machines were dismantled so they could be transported to India by sea. Flight Lieutenant David McIntyre was chosen to pilot the second aeroplane, and his passenger was a cameraman employed by a film company called Gaumont British News to make a movie of this remarkable flight over what the newspapers called 'the roof of the world'.

The journey to the north-east of India took several weeks, but both aircraft and their crews were ready to fly by the start of April. This is when the weather conditions in the Himalayas are slightly better than at other times of the year, and on 3 April 1933 the pilots took off from Purnia and flew towards their target.

The two Westlands had been chosen for their ability to climb very fast after take-off, because the pilots and their passengers knew that they wouldn't survive flying in the cold,

thin air for very long. However, even before reaching Everest, one of the passengers was in trouble. Cameraman Sidney Bonnett was having difficulty breathing because his oxygen mask had a crack in it. He tried to fix the leak by tying a handkerchief around it but is thought to have then lost consciousness before the pilot realised what had happened.

In fact, the pilots were also having problems. After being blown off course, Douglas-Hamilton realised that both aircraft were trapped in a tremendous down-rush of air coming off the mountain. As fast as the Westlands tried to fly upwards, the ferocious, buffeting wind forced them back down again.

McIntyre's aircraft was apparently saved by a sudden, unexpected upward rush of air, and Douglas-Hamilton refused to discuss how close he had come to smashing into a rock face during his own grim struggle. It was, he said later, something he preferred not to think about ever again. But eventually the two machines made it over the summit.

The pilots still had enough fuel and oxygen in their tanks to circle the peak for a few minutes before turning for home. The cameraman was too ill to continue filming, but he survived, and during a second flight two weeks later Douglas-Hamilton's passenger managed to take some spectacular photographs of the cold, dangerous slopes leading up to the summit.

Unfortunately, when news of the team's success reached London, *The Times* newspaper accidentally printed a picture of the wrong mountain. The correct photographs did prove

useful in the end, however, as they were used to plot a new route to the summit that allowed Everest to finally be climbed twenty years later.

Amelia Earhart

Vanishing Without a Trace (Pacific Ocean, 1937)

The first time Amelia Earhart flew across the Atlantic it was as a passenger, not a pilot, but in 1928 that was enough to make the headlines because she was the first woman in the world to have made the journey. Earhart clearly wanted more than fame, however, and quickly decided to do it again, only this time with herself at the controls.

She'd learned to fly in her early twenties and had bought her own second-hand aeroplane just a few months later. (This was bright yellow and nicknamed 'The Canary'.) Although she had trained as an army nurse and then become a social worker helping migrants, flying was her real passion in life. She knew she was good at it too and soon demonstrated her skill and courage by climbing to a record height of more than 5.5 kilometres. She did this in a machine called an autogyro, a forerunner of the modern helicopter.

By 1932 the trail-blazing Earhart was looking for a new adventure, one she felt would justify her fame as an aviator, and on 20 May that year she took off from Newfoundland in

Canada in a gleaming red Lockheed Vega. Several people had already pointed out that she looked a lot like Charles Lindbergh, and now Earhart was determined to fly cross the Atlantic Ocean on her own, just as he had a few years earlier.

The sturdy Vega was a much larger aircraft than Lindbergh's tiny *Spirit of St Louis*, and this certainly helped her smash his record by touching down in Northern Ireland in less than half the time he had spent airborne in 1927. The flight was nevertheless a remarkable achievement, and Earhart's fame soared even higher when people learned how she had battled strong northerly winds, icy conditions and numerous mechanical problems.

Earhart was soon busy travelling around Europe and America, giving inspirational talks to large, fascinated audiences and encouraging as many women as possible to take up flying. As only the second person to fly the Atlantic alone she was also presented with various medals and prestigious awards wherever she went.

Earhart's reputation was enhanced even further when, a few months later, she became the first woman in the world to fly across the whole of America. Coast to coast, this involved taking the Vega an even greater distance than from Canada to Ireland: an amazing 3,938 kilometres, as opposed to 3,260. At the time this was longest non-stop flight by a female pilot, but it still wasn't enough for Earhart. Even having notched up these impressive records, she was still obsessed with the idea of showing the world that she was one of its greatest-ever pilots.

Her determination grew even stronger the following year, when newspaper headlines announced that a one-eyed Native American called Wiley Post had managed to fly, alone, right around the world. In the 1930s it was impossible to circumnavigate the globe without stopping many times to refuel, but Post had somehow managed to do it incredibly quickly, to try to set a record that was unlikely to be beaten for a long time. As a result, and despite taking off without some much-needed maps, he had completed the epic 25,000-kilometre journey in just seven days, eighteen hours and forty-nine minutes. The only previous attempt to circle the globe, in an airship, had taken its German crew almost three times as long.

Wiley had made his momentous flight in *Winnie Mae*, a Lockheed Vega like Earhart's, and after studying the details of his flight she decided she wanted to attempt something similar. This time she chose a slightly larger aircraft called an Electra and selected a crew of three to navigate and operate the all-important radio while she concentrated on flying.

Unfortunately, it took Earhart a long time to get the necessary funding, and when everything was finally ready in March 1937 her first attempt began so badly that she had no alternative but to call it off. The first problem was a serious mechanical fault with the Electra's twin engines. This had worsened over the Pacific, and after touching down on the island of Hawaii to refuel the aircraft had to spend a full three days in a US Navy workshop at Pearl Harbor. The frustration must have been tremendous for Earhart and her crew, but

93

then, once the Electra was repaired and cleared for take-off, things got even worse. This time the aircraft spun out of control before it had even left the runway, possibly due to a tyre bursting or as the result of pilot error.

No one was hurt, but the Electra was badly damaged. Earhart had to delay the flight yet again while the broken aircraft was shipped back to California to be rebuilt. It took until June before everything was ready for a second attempt, by which time the pilot had decided to try flying the other way around the globe. She was convinced that the winds and weather would be more favourable travelling from west to east and had also decided to take along only one companion, her navigator, Fred Noonan.

The Electra took off from Miami on 1 June, and after making numerous refuelling stops in South America, Africa and south-east Asia, it touched down four weeks later on the Indonesian island of New Guinea. By this time the pair had completed **35,000 kilometres of their momentous journey**, and all without serious incident. This meant Earhart and Noonan had already flown a far greater distance than Post's total of 24,903 kilometres, yet the most dangerous part of their flight still lay ahead. This would involve crossing the Pacific, which at almost 170 million square kilometres is by far the largest ocean on Earth. The navigational challenges of crossing such a vast area were considerable. There were hardly any landmarks to help Noonan plot the last 11,000 kilometres of their journey and very few emergency runways if something went wrong again with the Electra.

Undeterred, the pair refuelled the aircraft and took off the following morning. They were heading for Howland Island, a remote, uninhabited speck of land lying just north of the equator. The weather was good and the 4,100-kilometre journey was expected to take the Electra around twenty hours, but neither Earhart nor Noonan was ever seen again.

Nearly ninety years later still no one knows what went wrong, although there are plenty of theories. These include Earhart landing on the wrong island, where the pair starved to death, or their being captured as spies by the Japanese, who went on to declare war on the US a few years later. It has even been suggested that they found their way back to America without anyone knowing and lived out the rest of their lives under false identities.

It's hard to imagine why they would have done this, but by far the most bizarre idea is that Earhart and her navigator were kidnapped by aliens while crossing an area of the Pacific known as the Bermuda Triangle. People have linked this to several mysterious disappearances over the years, but as there is no evidence to support it most aviation experts think Earhart probably just lost her way and the Electra ran out of fuel before crashing down into the Pacific.

It was a tragic end for this remarkable pioneer. While it's true that the mystery surrounding her disappearance has made Amelia Earhart history's most famous female pilot, she deserves to be remembered more for her achievements than for her sad and untimely death.

Empire C-Class

Crash of a Flying Giant (Belgian Congo, 1939)

By the 1920s Britain had the largest empire the world had ever seen. Incorporating more than fifty countries in Europe, Asia, Africa and the Americas, it covered a quarter of the world's surface. It was home to at least a quarter of the people on Earth, but being ruled from London was sometimes unpopular and most countries in the empire eventually became independent.

Transport around such a vast area was slow and extremely difficult. The distances involved were enormous, and many parts of the world still didn't have the wide, well-made roads, runways and railways which today we think of as normal. One answer to this problem was to travel in the flying boats owned and flown by Imperial Airways of London.

The company's Empire C-Class machines could take off and land on water, just like the Schneider Trophy-winning seaplanes. They were spacious and technologically highly advanced, and they provided a luxurious way for passengers to travel from one side of the world to the other. Passengers could enjoy six-course dinners and fantastic views through the aircraft's large picture windows. From the pilots' point of view, landing on the seemingly endless expanse of Africa's Lake Victoria must have been like having a runway almost the length of Ireland.

A jokey signpost at the entrance to one British airport gave passengers an idea of what to expect. The sign read 'CAIRO 2,000 MILES – KARACHI 4,000 MILES – JOHANNESBURG 6,000 MILES – SYDNEY 11,000 MILES' – all names which must have sounded strange and exciting at a time when most people in Britain had never even crossed the English Channel to get to France. Journey times were long by modern standards, but most were measured in days rather than weeks (or even months), which is how long those same trips would have taken by ship.

Before long, Imperial Airways had the largest flying-boat fleet in the world and its pilots were flying nearly a million kilometres every month. **The company carried 70,000 passengers a year**, as well as hundreds of tonnes of urgent post and even treasure in the form of solid gold bars. Its longest route was from Britain to New Zealand, but then in September 1939 everything suddenly changed with the start of World War II.

Britain raced to get as many of its aircraft back home as possible, and most of the flying boats were quickly converted for military service with the RAF and Britain's allies.

Unfortunately, one of them, called *Corsair*, got stuck in Africa because its crew had lost their way and then almost run out of fuel. `With only minutes to spare before its tanks ran dry`, *Corsair*'s pilot had managed to land on a small river in a remote, swampy part of what was then called the Belgian Congo. No one was injured, but a rock just beneath the surface of the muddy water tore an eight-metre hole in the body of the aircraft.

The shallow Dungu River was barely wider than *Corsair*'s wingspan, which meant that the pilot would have struggled to take off again even if he had any fuel. The aircraft had to be rescued and brought back somehow, though. Even a damaged C-Class was much too valuable to be abandoned, and the manufacturer told Imperial it had no plans to build any replacements as it had already begun making bombers to help win the war.

Back in London, the airline decided to fly a team of engineers out to Africa. Their job would be to repair and refloat the aircraft, and then find a way to get it back into the air. This was much harder than it sounds, and eventually so many local people were employed to help rescue the aircraft that a whole new village had to be built on the banks of the Dungu to accommodate them. The villagers called their new village Corsairville in honour of the ill-fated aircraft.

Unfortunately, none of the engineers could speak the local Bangala language, which made everyone's job even harder, and conditions in the village were difficult for them. Food was so scarce that they sometimes ate snake sandwiches, and the hot, humid air buzzed all day and night with the sound of millions of stinging, biting insects. In the end it took more than three months for them to haul the 19-tonne wreck out of the water and for the hole in its hull to be patched up.

Even once *Corsair* had been refloated and made ready to fly, taking off was going to be difficult and highly dangerous. A series of heavy thunderstorms meant the river was slightly deeper than normal, but it was still very narrow and lined with trees that were tall enough to damage the wings. The Dungu also had a dangerous bend in it which the pilot would have to turn through while accelerating to take off.

The local workforce was paid to cut down trees along the river and clear as much vegetation as it could from the water. The tail of the C-Class was then tied to a tree stump using a thick rope. This was so that the four engines could reach full power. Only then would the rope be released so that the aeroplane could roar off down the river at maximum speed.

It seemed like a good plan, but as the pilot accelerated towards the bend in the river he realised he wasn't going anywhere near fast enough to take off. He quickly switched off the engines and almost immediately collided with the same submerged rock as before. This ripped a second huge gash in the newly repaired hull.

Three months' work had been destroyed in a moment,

but the engineers knew they had no choice other than to start all over again. This time it would be even tougher. Everyone was exhausted and they knew that the river level would soon begin to lower again in the scorching sun. Another run along it was too risky, so the engineers decided to build a dam all the way across the river, from one side to the other. A solid wall of wood and stone would make the river flood and create a large artificial lake. Once this was deep enough, they hoped, *Corsair* would be able take off in the normal way.

The dam needed to be huge, though, more than 70 metres from end to end, so while one team set to work repairing the damaged hull, another began laying a new road through the swamp. This was needed to bring in supplies of heavy timber called ironwood from nearly 50 kilometres away.

The ironwood was needed to build the dam, which would then be strengthened using 300 tonnes of rock pulled from the river and the surrounding swamp. Any rocks which were too heavy or impossible to move were clearly marked in order to prevent a third accident. Once the dam was finished the lake slowly began to form. By January, **a full ten months after** *Corsair* had made its unfortunate landing, the water looked deep enough to make another attempt.

Once again the aeroplane's tail was roped to a tree stump, and with a new pilot seated at the controls its four powerful engines roared noisily into action. Hundreds of people had walked for hours to watch as the aeroplane slipped free of the rope and its pilot powered his machine across the brand-new lake. Moments later *Corsair* lifted off the water and, after dipping its wings as a thanks and farewell to everyone down below, set a course for home.

Happily, the crew made it back safely, and the flying boat spent the rest of World War II carrying essential supplies and military personnel. By the time the last of these fabulous machines was taken out of service in 1947, this particular one had flown `more than three-quarters of a million kilometres`.

The Attagirls

'I Flew 400 Spitfires' (UK, 1940)

Thousands of women joined the RAF when it was formed in 1918. They did many different jobs as drivers, skilled flight mechanics and air traffic controllers, but it took nearly seventy-five years before the RAF allowed any of its female officers to train as pilots.

Despite the unfairness of this, women who could afford to often paid for their own flying lessons, and many of them went on to play an important role in World War II. Nearly 170 belonged to an organisation called the Air Transport Auxiliary (ATA). Their work involved flying military aircraft, mostly around the British Isles: for example, from the factories where new aircraft were built to the airfields where they were needed most. At other times the ATA flew badly damaged aircraft back to factories and maintenance units, where they could be repaired.

The organisation also employed male pilots, many of whom were disabled or considered unfit or too old to fly in the RAF. Because of this, people used to joke that ATA stood for

'Ancient and Tattered Airmen'. Most of the men and women were British, but foreign pilots also joined the ATA from more than two dozen other countries. These included Canada, the US, Australia, New Zealand, South Africa, India, Russia and China.

The work of the ATA was crucial because it meant that the RAF's own pilots could concentrate on fighting the war. There were still members of the public who disapproved of women flying, but a country at war needs all the pilots it can get. In fact, some of these women had much more experience of flying than a lot of the young men in the RAF. Pauline Gower, for example, had already flown more than 2,000 hours before she joined the ATA, and Joan Hughes had started flying when she was only fifteen. Both of them knew that the RAF was having to rush very young male pilots through training because it needed to replace more senior officers who had crashed or been shot down.

ATA's first eight women recruits were followed by a varied bunch of volunteers that included a ballet dancer, an Essex farmer, an Olympic skier, a hairdresser **and at least one grandmother**. Three more women joined after making a daring escape from Poland after their country was invaded by Germany. One American volunteer had already flown more than 4,000 hours before signing up, but to begin with even the most experienced women were not allowed to fly anything other than small, single-engine aircraft. They were also paid a lot less than the men doing the same job, although this was later corrected.

By the end of the war the women of the ATA had flown nearly 150 different types of

aeroplane and they were affectionately referred to as 'the Attagirls'. These planes ranged from single-seat fighters such as the Spitfire and Hurricane to four-engine 'heavies' like the famous Avro Lancaster and B-17 Flying Fortress. This extraordinary variety explains the ATA's other nickname, which was 'Anything To Anywhere'.

One pilot, Lettice Curtis, delivered a Spitfire, a twin-engine Mosquito, an American Mitchell and then a huge Stirling bomber – `all in a single day`. Another, Mary Ellis, flew more than a thousand aircraft during her time with the ATA, including a record 400 Spitfires and a Gloster Meteor, Britain's first-ever jet fighter. Similarly, Margot Duhalde, who had terrible eyesight and could hardly speak English when she arrived from Chile, went on to fly seventy different types of aircraft to RAF squadrons based in France, Belgium and the Netherlands.

These examples were not unusual for someone in the ATA, and many of the pilots had quite extraordinary stories of their own. One was a member of Thailand's royal family; another was an ex-racing driver who'd broken the world land speed record no fewer than three times. Duhalde herself had spent several nights in jail after being mistaken for an enemy spy when she first arrived in London and attempted to volunteer.

The newspapers published many fascinating articles about courageous young aviators such as Joy and Yvonne Gough, two sisters who had never even flown as passengers before becoming pilots. Other female flyers were already very well known long before they joined

the ATA. Winnie Crossley, for example, had spent five years working as a stunt pilot and barnstormer, giving thrilling flying demonstrations, and in 1930 Amy Johnson had made headlines around the world when she became the first woman to fly solo from Britain to Australia.

Jacqueline Cochran was another of the organisation's celebrities. She had learned to fly in under three weeks and went on to win numerous air races, as well as break several international records. She was also the first woman to fly a bomber across the Atlantic, and like Johnson, her achievements did a lot to encourage a whole generation of young women to fly.

Many ATA pilots had already lost brothers, husbands and best friends in the fighting before joining up. They knew that delivering an aircraft was safer than flying one in combat, but ferrying anything to anywhere was still a highly dangerous career move. These women all had to fly long distances without a radio or any working weapons. The job was lonely and highly stressful, and they often had to travel hundreds of kilometres in a completely new type of aircraft that they had never seen before. Whenever this happened, with an urgent deadline to keep and only a basic map and a compass, pilots had no choice but to take off and then try to figure out how to fly the machine along the way.

In less than five years, `the ATA successfully delivered an astonishing 309,000 aircraft this way`. Many of its pilots

went on to have successful careers in aviation, but 173 men and women lost their lives while doing their duty. They included Amy Johnson, who tragically drowned after parachuting into the freezing River Thames when she ran out of fuel in thick fog. Eleven more were killed during a German torpedo attack. Others died in mid-air collisions, forced landings and fires, or simply as a result of flying an unfamiliar, faulty or badly damaged aircraft in the most atrocious weather.

Sadly, Johnson's body was never found, but in 1950 a special memorial to her and her ATA colleagues was unveiled in St Paul's Cathedral in London to ensure that **these remarkable women would never be forgotten**.

Night Witches

The First Female Fighter Pilots (Russia, 1941)

Britain wasn't the only country that refused to allow women pilots to join its air force. The same was true of every country fighting in World War II, until female pilots in Russia and the rest of the Soviet Union eventually managed to win the right to equal treatment.

There were already plenty of female Russian pilots when four million German troops invaded their country in 1941. This was the largest invading army in history, but when some of the women tried to volunteer as fighter pilots they were given excuses and piles of seemingly pointless forms to fill in. This was probably done in the hope that they would get fed up and go away, even though tens of thousands of Russian women were already serving in their country's armed forces.

Marina Raskova refused to accept defeat. She had been the first Russian woman to qualify as an air navigator and the country's first-ever female military flying instructor. This meant she was paid by the government to teach men how to become fighter

pilots, so it was completely ridiculous that she was unable to be one herself. Fortunately, the Russian leader, Josef Stalin, was a great admirer of Raskova. She used their friendship to persuade him to give pilots like her the same opportunities as men. It took a while, but eventually Stalin agreed to the formation of three new all-female air regiments.

This was the first time anything like this had happened anywhere in the world. Not only would the pilots and navigators in these regiments be women but so would the support staff, including all the engineers and ground crew. **More than 2,000 women immediately applied to join**, and nearly all of those who were accepted were aged between seventeen and twenty-six.

Before long one of units, the 586th Fighter Aviation Regiment, had produced the world's first two female air 'aces', the name given to pilots who shot down five or more enemy aircraft. These two pilots, Lydia Litvyak and Yekaterina Budanova, had both learned how to fly as teenagers and now found themselves piloting fast, reliable machines called Yak-1s.

When Litvyak shot down her first German aircraft the pilot was captured after parachuting down to the ground. He asked to meet the pilot who had beaten him and was shocked to see that it was a woman. He refused to believe she was really a pilot and thought the Russians were having a joke at his expense. Budanova, meanwhile, took part in several ferocious attacks against both fighters and bombers. On two separate occasions she managed to shoot down two aircraft in a single day.

The second unit was the 587th Bomber Aviation Regiment. This was commanded by Marina Raskova personally, and its pilots were equipped with the very latest type of aircraft, a twin-engine dive bomber called the Petlyakov Pe-2. The women took part in more than a thousand air raids and dropped nearly 900 tonnes of high explosives on many different enemy targets. Raskova herself was killed in 1943, but five of her comrades survived and were made Heroes of the Soviet Union, the country's very highest honour.

Many male pilots were furious that Raskova and her regiment were allowed to fly the newest and most advanced aircraft available. They must have been delighted to see that the opposite was true of the pilots in Stalin's third all-female unit. Instead, the members of the 588th Night Bomber Aviation Regiment had to make do with second-hand uniforms and oversized men's boots, which they stuffed with torn-up bedsheets to make them fit. The regiment was also given some of the oldest, cheapest and most unimpressive flying machines that the Soviet armed forces possessed. Their Polikarpov U-2s were simple biplanes. This meant they had two wings stacked one on top of the other and were made of plywood and a kind of cotton fabric called canvas. The U-2 looked like something left over from World War I, and its top speed of only 152 kph meant that by the 1940s it was one of the slowest aircraft anywhere in the world. Raskova's Pe-2s were almost four times faster, yet despite their hopeless equipment the U-2 pilots soon became widely feared by their German opponents.

There were never that many of them, just forty two-person crews, but their success in battle helped them become famous enough for the German army to promise a special medal to any soldier who managed to shoot down one of their aircraft. The Germans also had a nickname for them: *Nachthexen*, meaning 'Night Witches', because of a brilliant tactic the women devised to reduce the chances of their slow and underpowered aircraft being shot down.

Their missions always took place at night, and the women became expert at gliding towards their target with their engines idling or even shut down completely. This kept the noise to a minimum and made it hard for anyone to hear the U-2s coming, until it was too late and the women had begun dropping their bombs. This trick meant that in the final stages of an attack the loudest noise to be heard was just a soft whooshing sound as the wind rushed over the aircraft's wings. This was a highly effective tactic and extremely unnerving for the Germans, who compared each new attack to witches swooping down on their broomsticks. It was this that gave rise to the regiment's sinister nickname, something which delighted all the women involved in carrying out the raids.

However, because the U-2 was small and underpowered, it could carry only six bombs at a time, three under each wing. To make up for this, women like Yekaterina Ryabova and Nadezhda Popova got used to flying eight or more missions each night. Popova's record is thought to be eighteen, which must have been incredibly exhausting because, even flying under cover of darkness, the risks the women took were enormous.

Popova was only nineteen when she flew her first mission, but she went on to complete more than 850 of them in Belarus, Poland and Germany. Flying low was always dangerous, and when she landed after one successful attack she counted no fewer than forty-two bullet holes in her aircraft, map and flying helmet. In another raid she was shot down but survived. Besides enemy gunfire, freezing winds were another constant danger, as these threatened to tear apart the fragile little U-2s. Sitting in open cockpits dressed in ill-fitting uniforms (and with no parachutes), the women were also at serious risk of frostbite.

When Germany was finally defeated in 1945, all three regiments were quickly disbanded, despite their huge success. By the end of the war an impressive 800,000 Russian women had served with the Soviet army and air force, and the records show that the Night Witches had been awarded `more medals than any other female unit`. These brave, pioneering pilots had flown an estimated 30,000 missions and dropped more than 20,000 tonnes of bombs on the invading Germany army. They had also shown the world that women could fly – and fight – just as well as men.

Colditz Cock

An Incredible Escape Attempt (Germany, 1944)

More than eight million soldiers, sailors and airmen surrendered or were captured during World War II, including around 170,000 members of the British armed forces. Most of them became prisoners of war (or POWs) and had to spend months or even years in special camps patrolled by armed guards.

The most famous camp was Oflag IV-C in eastern Germany. Most of the inmates called it Colditz Castle, which was the name of the main building at the camp. At first this ancient fortress housed prisoners from Poland, France, Belgium, the Netherlands and Canada. However, in 1943 it was decided to use it for British and American officers only, especially those the Germans thought were most likely to try to escape.

Breaking out of any POW camp was difficult and dangerous. Even if prisoners were able to dig a tunnel without being detected or climb over the high barbed-wire fences, they still found themselves thousands of kilometres from home, in a hostile country where most of

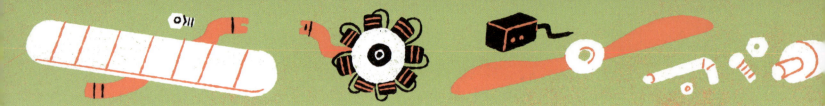

them couldn't speak the local language.

Prisoners knew that travelling any distance across Europe in wartime was almost impossible without the right documents or money and friends to help. Friendly Germans were particularly hard to find because people living near the camps were warned that they would be executed if they were caught helping a foreigner to get out of Germany. Even so, thousands of prisoners tried to escape, and approximately 1,200 were successful and made it back to Britain. Prisoners called this a 'home run', but in reality most of those who escaped under the wire or over it were quickly recaptured and returned to their camps. German army commanders found the whole thing infuriating because they had to waste so much time and effort in tracking down escaped POWs, many of whom would simply try again.

Colditz was therefore intended to be even more secure than an ordinary POW camp. The original, imposing fortress had been built almost a thousand years earlier on a steep hill above a vertical rock face nearly 75 metres high. Most other camps were just a series of large wooden huts surrounded by wire fences, but the high exterior walls at Colditz were at least two metres thick. There were also many more armed guards than at an ordinary camp, and the Zwickauer Mulde river at the bottom of the cliff formed another barrier which any escapees had to cross.

However, the Germans had overlooked one very important thing. Although the castle had some famous prisoners (including the founder of the SAS and two of King George VI's

nephews), most of the inmates were sent to Colditz because they were very good at escaping. As a result of this the castle soon became a sort of school of escapology.

Prisoners who had escaped and then been recaptured were happy to share their experiences with their comrades. Between them they also developed a lot of clever techniques that could be useful to anyone making another escape attempt. In hidden corners of the castle skilled inmates began making duplicate keys for some of the castle doors and manufacturing useful tools out of cutlery and metal bucket handles. Others produced copies of maps showing escape routes out of Germany or forged the identity papers that even an ordinary German needed to travel around the country.

Although the Germans had expected the number of escape attempts to fall, these activities actually led to an increase. They also helped to inspire one of the most extraordinary escape plans of the entire war. This involved the creation of a fabulous device that the prisoners called the Colditz Cock, a working, full-size flying machine which was `designed to allow two POWs to fly off the castle roof and right over its walls`.

The idea for this had come from Tony Rolt, an officer in the Rifle Brigade. More than half a century earlier the castle had been home to a man called Georg Baumgarten. He had built some of the first airships in Germany, but Rolt convinced the other prisoners that a glider would be a more practical means of escape.

Rolt had noticed that the roof of the castle's chapel wasn't overlooked by any of the guard posts. He thought that it was high enough to act as a launch pad for a small glider that could fly two men over the walls and the river to freedom. Rolt was also convinced that because so many escape attempts involved tunnels, the guards spent more time inspecting the parts of the castle which were underground than looking up at the roof.

Naturally, once Rolt's plan had been accepted, `everything had to be done in total secrecy`. A false wall was carefully constructed in one of the castle's attics to conceal a tiny workshop, and a system of look-outs and alarms was organised to warn if any guards were nearby. Anything the team needed to build the glider had to be stolen and smuggled up to the attic without the Germans noticing. Even the men's woodworking tools had to be made from scratch. Ordinary nails were cleverly turned into hand-powered drills, and the metal spring from a wind-up record player was used to make some tiny saw blades.

One of the prisoners had been a member of the London Glider Club before the war, and he helped two army engineers with the basic design. The men were also lucky enough to find a book in the castle library which described how to build an aircraft. Even more surprising was that the book was written in English.

The framework for the glider's body was built up using wooden slats from the men's beds and then covered with cotton material recycled from sheets and sleeping bags. Several

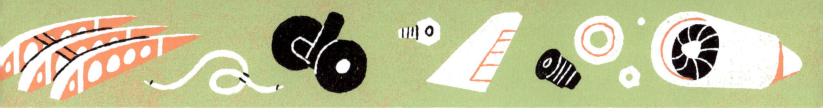

floorboards were removed from areas of the castle which the guards missed on their inspections. These were used to make the wings, and electric wiring carefully stripped from the walls became cables for controlling the angle of the wings once the Cock was flying.

The team also had to find a way of launching the six-metre-long glider off the chapel roof. They came up with an extraordinary scheme that was a bit like the Wright brothers' Grand Junction Railroad. This involved building a sloping 'runway' on the roof out of tables, and then using ropes and pulleys attached to a heavy metal bath full of concrete. When the bath was pushed off the chapel roof, the rope would pull the glider down the runway at `a speed of approximately 50 kph`. The army engineers' careful calculations indicated that this would be fast enough to launch the glider, but sadly it was never put to the test. Having to work in secret, and with home-made tools, meant that the Colditz Cock had taken too long to build. By the time it was completed the US Army had successfully invaded this part of Germany and set the men free.

The prisoners must have been delighted that the war was over, but it is a pity that the machine they had worked on for so long never got to fly. Luckily, one of the Americans took a photograph of it up in the attic, because the Colditz Cock disappeared soon afterwards – no one knows how or where it went – and it was never seen again.

It wasn't just the men themselves who found the mystery frustrating, and decades later a company in Britain built an exact copy to see whether or not the original could really have

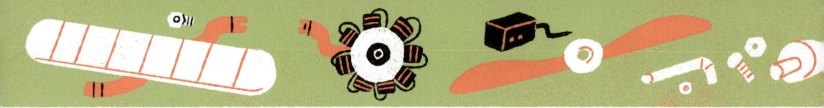

flown. The results were spectacular, and after several successful test flights that proved the real one would have worked the replica Cock was preserved and put on permanent display in a museum in Hampshire.

Lothar Sieber

The Tragic Human Firework (Germany, 1945)

Two world wars led to the rapid development of many new, improved aircraft. Each side in these conflicts was desperate to defeat the other, and aeroplane manufacturers quickly learned that every government would pay for anything that looked like it might give their own country a crucial military advantage over their enemies.

By the mid-1940s bombers and fighter aircraft were faster and better equipped than ever before, but government money paid for some impressive new inventions too. These included the first-ever jet-powered aircraft and enormous, unmanned rockets that could fly so fast that no one could see them coming.

The jet engine was a British invention, but some of the most extraordinary designs were developed in Germany. Fortunately, by the time they were ready to go into combat, it already looked as though Hitler would lose the war. Most historians think Germany's military leaders knew they couldn't win using conventional weapons and so decided to take a

desperate gamble by trying something completely different. The Germans called the results *Wunderwaffen*, or 'wonder weapons'. They were designed to defend Germany's towns and cities from the increasing number of devastating raids by the RAF and US Air Force. However, most *Wunderwaffen* turned out to be hopeless failures, and the bombing raids continued.

For many years after the war people believed that German scientists `had managed to build a kind of flying saucer`, but there is no evidence that this actually happened. The Horten Ho 229 was certainly real, however, a strange, triangular aircraft with no body or tail fin. Aviation engineers call this kind of design a 'flying wing' because that's what it looks like, but they are much harder to control than a normal aeroplane. In 1944 the Germans' first one caught fire and crashed during a test flight, killing the pilot. The only other prototype was captured by the US Army before it could be sent into battle.

Another wacky design had a circular wing, but this was even worse than the triangle. It was called the Sack AS-6 and managed only a few short 'hops' down the runway instead of taking off. The inventor, a farmer, was convinced he could make the improvements needed for it to fly properly, but before he had a chance to try it was destroyed in an American raid on the airfield.

Although these particular ideas now seem a bit ridiculous, Germany's rocket scientists had some successes. A lot of their work was far more advanced than anything being done by

rivals in Britain, America and Russia, and they demonstrated this by building the terrifying V-2 missile and the world's first rocket-powered fighter. The latter, the Messerschmitt Me 163 Komet, was actually the fastest aircraft of the entire war. It had at least twice the power of any British or American fighter, although it was very difficult to fly or land safely and ran out of fuel after only eight or nine minutes. Even the most skilled pilots said they had trouble controlling the Komet at speeds of nearly 1,000 kph, and the body of at least one airman actually dissolved when some of its special, highly corrosive fuel leaked into his cockpit.

Despite these difficulties, Komets successfully attacked and destroyed nine American and British aircraft. However, at least a dozen of them were shot down while doing this or simply crashed. Others made such bad landings that the pilots were injured and couldn't fly again for months or even years. The new technology had looked very promising, but even for a country as desperate as Germany was aeroplanes as dangerous as the Komet really didn't make much sense.

Because of this **the Komet is still the only rocket-powered aeroplane ever to be used in combat**, but if anything the Bachem Ba 349 was even stranger and more dangerous. Komets at least looked like aeroplanes and took off in much the same way. The Ba 349 was more of a gigantic firework, and like a firework it was designed to shoot up vertically at the most incredible speed.

The machine was at least cheap and easy to build, but then it needed to be because each

launch caused so much damage to the rocket that it couldn't be flown again. Taking off like a firework gave it an important advantage, though, because it avoided the need for runways, at a time when German airfields were being attacked and destroyed nearly every day.

Once launched, the pilot didn't have to do anything until he spotted some enemy aircraft in the distance. Instead of guns, he had two dozen smaller rockets in the nose which could then be fired in their direction. These flew far too quickly for anyone to shoot them down, and far too quickly for an enemy pilot to get out of the way. Once they had all been fired, the Ba 349 pilot parachuted to safety and the remains of the rocket simply fell to the ground.

That was the plan anyway, but only one pilot ever got to fly a Ba 349, and his short flight was far from successful. Lothar Sieber had almost lost his air force job after being caught drunk on duty, but at twenty-two years old he was regarded as a skilled and experienced pilot. This may explain why he was chosen for the Ba 349's first and only flight, or he may just have been a very unlucky man.

On 1 March 1945 Sieber climbed into the machine, strapped himself in and waited for the terrifying rush as the rocket's motors ignited with a deafening roar. No one knows exactly what went wrong. Theoretically, the Ba 349 was so fast that it could have reached the top of Everest in under a minute, but within seconds of the launch it was clear that both man and machine were in terrible trouble. Observers on the ground saw a small piece of the rocket break off, before the rest of it disappeared into the clouds. They waited nervously,

hoping to see Sieber's parachute, but instead the rocket reappeared moments later. It was pointing downwards as it came screaming out of the clouds, and it piled into the ground at an incredible speed.

The test flight had lasted only seconds, and worryingly there was no sign at all of Sieber in the five-metre-deep crater at the crash site. Eventually, only an arm and a part of one leg were recovered from the wreckage . . .

Perhaps the most surprising thing about this story is that even after this gruesome outcome, several other pilots volunteered to give the doomed device another try. Some even offered to kill themselves by piloting rockets which were designed to ram enemy aircraft in mid-air. But fortunately the war ended when Germany surrendered in May 1945. This brought an end to their experiments with these dangerous human fireworks, although many new and exciting aircraft designs continued to appear.

Chuck Yeager

Flying Faster Than a Bullet (US, 1947)

By the end of World War II the most advanced versions of the British Spitfire and American P-51 Mustang could fly at speeds of around 700 kph. This was almost 50 per cent faster than any fighter could achieve at the start of the conflict six years earlier, and flying speeds continued to increase once the war ended.

An important new target for many designers, pilots and engineers was the speed of sound, or 'Mach 1'. This is the speed at which sound travels from one point to another, and it is just over 1,000 kph. That's equivalent to travelling nearly 280 metres every second (or about three times the speed of a Formula 1 car), although it varies slightly depending on the air temperature and the altitude at which the pilot is flying.

Anything that can fly this fast is referred to as supersonic. It's hard to believe, but the end of a whip travels faster than the speed of sound when the whip is cracked. Many of the millions of artillery shells fired during World War I were also supersonic, but achieving a similar speed

in an aeroplane is very difficult, which is why no one had managed it by the mid-1940s. At such high speeds the stresses on the aircraft's bodywork and wings – and on the pilot – would be enormous, and something called drag (which slows down an aircraft) also increases as aircraft travel faster and faster.

Although many German pilots had been killed or badly injured flying rocket-powered aircraft during World War II, many experts still thought rocket technology was the best way to overcome these problems. This was especially true in the US, where researchers were interested in developing faster and faster military aircraft, as well as exploring the exciting possibility of **sending humans to the edge of space**.

The British had already designed an aircraft to do this during the war, but the government cancelled the project once Germany had been defeated. This was done to save money, and it meant the top-secret plane was never completed or flown. Instead, the plans for it were shared with the Americans, which may explain how the Bell Aircraft company managed to produced something very similar-looking in 1946.

Bell called its rocket-powered prototype the X-1. It was the first in a series of so-called X-planes, which are still some of the fastest aircraft ever produced. This particular one is by far the most famous because its pilot, Charles 'Chuck' Yeager, used it to become the first person in the world to successfully fly at supersonic speed.

Bell's bright orange X-1 was described at the time as a 'bullet with wings', and it had only one purpose, which was to fly very, very fast. For this reason, it wasn't equipped with any missiles, guns or bombs, and there was no room in the cockpit for anyone except Yeager. Its fuel was highly explosive liquefied oxygen.

Yeager was only twenty-four years old when he volunteered to fly the X-1, but he was already an exceptional pilot. When he was a teenager he had joined the US Army Air Force as an aircraft mechanic because he was too young to train as a pilot.

He waited a year and a half to learn to fly, but was then shot down in flames over France. He was lucky to survive and avoid capture, and after two months he managed to get back to England and rejoin his squadron in Suffolk. Shortly afterwards he became an 'ace' by shooting down an incredible five enemy aircraft in a single day.

Yeager was determined to continue flying after the war ended and quickly found a job as a military test pilot. This enabled him to fly more than 360 different types of aircraft, including many that had been captured from the Germans and Japanese. It is still an astonishing total, although nothing Yeager flew was ever quite as amazing as the Bell X-1.

Yeager was one of several highly experienced pilots who volunteered to fly the rocket-engined prototype. It took great courage because flying any new machine is potentially highly dangerous. This was especially true for the X-1, which was so different from a normal

fighter. In fact, many people didn't believe that flying at supersonic speed was even possible. Others thought that even if it was, the aeroplane and its pilot would be torn apart by the stresses involved.

An aircraft has to break something called the sound barrier to reach **supersonic speed**. This is when an aircraft flies fast enough for water droplets to form a strange, ghostly cloud around it. As it hits Mach 1, there is also a sudden loud explosion called a sonic boom. It's caused by soundwaves being forced into each other by the body of the aircraft speeding through the air, and the noise can be loud enough to shatter windows on the ground below and even damage walls. None of this happens with ordinary aeroplanes, and without trying to break the barrier it was impossible to be sure what the effects would be on the machine and the man inside it.

In October 1947 Yeager was selected to fly the X-1, even though he had recently broken several ribs falling off a horse. Even several days later he was still in too much pain to reach up to close the X-1's canopy after climbing into the cockpit. Instead, a gadget had to be hastily made out of an old broom handle so that he could perform this simple but essential task.

The X-1 wasn't designed to take off in the normal way, or even to be launched from the ground like a modern rocket. Instead, it was carried into the air inside the bomb bay of a Boeing B-29. This was a huge aeroplane just like the one used to drop the first atomic bombs at the end of World War II. When it reached 7,000 metres over the vast Mojave Desert in

California, the X-1 was released and Yeager's mission began.

At first, the X-1 fell through the air like an oversized bomb, until the pilot used its powerful rocket motor to soar to nearly 14,000 metres. Once the X-1 reached this 'test altitude', he accelerated to Mach 1 and then quickly went on to record an astonishing speed of 1,127 kph. Fuel runs out very rapidly at this speed, and moments later Yeager began his descent back to the desert, where he made a perfect landing on a dry lake bed.

Yeager had nicknamed the X-1 *Glamorous Glennis* after his wife, and he later described the experience of piloting it as 'nice, just like riding fast in a car'. Of course, he knew it was more than that, but because it was a secret military project, he wasn't allowed to talk to anyone about it. The public only found out about the historic achievement the following summer, when the X-1's story was leaked to a newspaper.

Yeager was hailed as a hero once the public was finally able to read about what had happened over the desert, but for him this was just the start. A few years later he flew another X-1 at nearly 2,600 kph, although he only narrowly avoided disaster this time when he lost control of the aircraft. **Yeager dropped a horrifying 16,000 metres in under a minute**, before managing to regain control and land safely. But even this brush with death didn't put him off breaking records, and he claimed several more for both speed and altitude over the next few years. He eventually retired in 1997, but nonetheless went on to make his final supersonic flight at the age of eighty-nine.

The de Havilland Comet

The Beginning of the Jet Age (UK, 1952)

Airline manufacturers continued making passenger planes with propellers after the war, but many air forces began to replace their front-line fighters and bombers with new aircraft powered by jet engines.

A jet engine draws air in at the front and compresses or squeezes it using spinning vanes or fins. The air is then combined with fuel and ignited, which greatly increases its volume. This forces it out of the rear of the engine at terrific speed, which in turn pushes the aircraft forward.

The technology made it possible for aircraft to fly much faster and higher than a plane with propellers, but it took several years before this made any difference to ordinary people. From the first jet fighter it took almost a decade for the first jet airliner to follow it into the sky. Even then, it was another three years before fare-paying passengers were invited on

board to enjoy the experience.

The airliner was the de Havilland Comet, a sleek, four-engine design with large rectangular picture windows and room for thirty-six passengers in its spacious cabin. A top speed of almost 800 kph made it at least 50 per cent faster than any of its rivals. This meant international journey times could be cut dramatically, something the aircraft quickly demonstrated by transporting forty-two passengers and crew from England to Rome, then Beirut and on to Khartoum, Entebbe, Livingstone and Johannesburg. A total of 10,800 kilometres, and all in under a day.

The Comet wasn't just fast, however. For the 20,000 spectators waiting to see it land at Johannesburg, it was also an exciting vision of the future. Passenger airliners in the early 1950s were slow, and most were very uncomfortable. Their old-fashioned piston engines were extremely noisy, and flying through stormy weather instead of above it could be a horrible experience for passengers. Many of these aircraft had been converted from cargo planes or even disused wartime bombers, and almost no consideration was given to passenger comfort, let alone luxury.

Compared to these, `the Comet looked like a spacecraft`, an engineering masterpiece with a mirror-like aluminium body and four powerful Ghost turbojets hidden in the swept-back wings. The cabins even had their own pressurised oxygen supply so the pilot could take it up to an altitude of 12 kilometres. This was far above any disruptive

storms and meant that Comet passengers could travel higher, faster, more smoothly and amid less noise than ever before, as well as enjoying stupendous views of the landscape far below.

The French and Americans were desperate to catch up with glamorous new jets of their own, but almost immediately disaster struck the British trailblazer. In October 1952 one of the Comets crashed at the end of the runway in Rome. Remarkably, no one was injured, but then a few months later another Comet crashed in Pakistan, killing everyone on board. Other terrible accidents occurred in Senegal, India and then over Italy.

By now the number of dead was almost a hundred passengers and aircrew, and all remaining Comets were promptly banned from taking off until an investigation had taken place. This revealed several problems, which were quickly put right, but then, just weeks afterwards, another Comet exploded in mid-air, killing twenty-one people.

A further, more thorough investigation was immediately ordered into what had gone wrong. This one involved placing the body of a Comet in a huge tank and filling the fuselage with water. The pressure of the water was then increased and decreased again and again to simulate the effects of approximately 9,000 hours of actual flying. The results of this test showed how the stresses on the aircraft's gleaming skin eventually caused it to break apart catastrophically.

Perhaps the only positive thing to come out of the episode is that aircraft accidents began to be investigated properly for the first time. It also meant the Comet had to be completely redesigned to become a larger, stronger and much safer aircraft. The new version was also more powerful thanks to its improved Rolls-Royce engines, and much smaller oval windows now replaced the original rectangular ones. All this took time to achieve, and the delay gave the rest of the airline industry the opportunity it needed to catch up and then, eventually, to overtake de Havilland.

In 1955 France unveiled the elegant, twin-engine Caravelle, which included many engineering ideas and technical features copied directly from the new, improved Comet. Three years later the first Boeing 707 took off in America. Neither was as handsome as the Comet (or as revolutionary as it had been in 1949), but the Comet's shocking safety record meant that its sales never recovered from the damaging headlines and the delay.

The Comet went on to make history again in 1958 by making the **first-ever transatlantic crossing** by a commercial jet airliner, and the last one was still flying nearly forty years later. However, the French managed to sell more than twice as many Caravelles in that time, and Boeing, similarly, sold nearly eight times as many of its larger, faster, better 707.

Others rivals followed, such as the Russian Tupolev Tu-104 and the Douglas DC-8. Once again, these weren't anywhere near as elegant as the British design, but they too outsold

it, in part because they could carry many more passengers even further, which made them cheaper to operate and more efficient to fly.

Very sadly, de Havilland never caught up. In 1956 the company had something else to celebrate when one of its pilots became the first man to fly at 1,000 miles an hour (1,600 kph), but even this wasn't enough. By 1960 de Havilland no longer existed as an independent aircraft manufacturer, but the pioneering Comet deserves to be remembered. It may have led the world for only a few short months, but it pointed the way to the future of fast, safe international travel for millions of ordinary people. In that sense it changed everything. Without de Havilland, the Caravelle might never have existed and many other magnificent machines, including the 707 and DC-8, would almost certainly have arrived far later than they did.

Gary Powers

Spies in the Sky (US, 1956)

Balloons and aeroplanes provided useful ways to observe troop movements during World War I, and in World War II Spitfires painted a special pink colour flew deep inside enemy territory looking for military bases and other top-secret sites.

The Spitfires were unusual because they had cameras instead of guns. Their pilots had orders to photograph anything suspicious, and the pink paint was thought to make the aircraft harder to spot against a blue or cloudy sky. Between them they took more than 20 million photographs, which were used to plan several major military operations, including the invasion of Europe (known as D-Day) and the famous Dambusters raid.

By the 1950s, however, things had moved on from the Spitfire. Aerial espionage had become far more sophisticated and now required an entirely new breed of specialised spy plane, one that incorporated some brilliant technology.

This was during a period called the Cold War, when the democratic nations of Western

Europe and the US found themselves allied against the communist countries of Eastern Europe and the Soviet Union. Each side felt threatened by the other, and this led to a dangerous escalation of military force. The two superpowers, Russia and America, never declared war on each other, but both began to build up huge stockpiles of nuclear weapons, which were powerful enough to destroy entire cities.

To begin with the Lockheed U-2 project was a way for the Americans to find out how great the threat from Russia was. Very little was known about the country at this time. Tourists were not welcome there, and for several years America and its allies had had to rely on photographs that had been captured from the Nazis at the end of the war. These were often very poor quality and badly out of date, so U-2 pilots were ordered to take new, better images while flying top-secret missions over Russia and, later, China, Vietnam and Cuba.

These flights were completely illegal, so it was vital that the public didn't know anything about the aircraft or its missions. Because everything had to be kept secret, the aircraft weren't built in the usual Lockheed factory but at a mysterious facility with the code name Skunk Works.

For the same reason, most of the missions had nothing to do with the US Air Force but were organised and even paid for by the CIA, America's secret service. The CIA was so determined to hide what it was up to that the first payment (equivalent to $12 million) was posted to the designer's home address instead of Lockheed's headquarters. Similarly, all

official documents carefully referred to the U-2 as an 'article' rather than an aeroplane, just in case any of the paperwork fell into enemy hands.

Naturally, the CIA also wanted its pilots to remain undetected when they were flying over enemy territory. Like the pink Spitfires, the U-2s were unarmed, and this meant they had no way to defend themselves if they were attacked by enemy aircraft or fired at from the ground. To help the pilots stay out of danger, the U-2 was engineered to fly at extremely high altitude. The Americans knew that Russia's newest supersonic fighters were capable of flying to a height of around 20,000 metres, so the U-2 was engineered to reach as high as 24,000 metres (that's almost 15 miles above the ground, or about three times higher than Mount Everest). It could also stay airborne for up to twelve hours, which was three or even four times longer than the U-2's Russian and Chinese adversaries.

The most amazing thing about the U-2, though, was its Hycon camera. This was the best high-resolution, high-altitude camera anywhere in the world in the 1950s. It was huge, larger than a fridge-freezer, and as a U-2 streaked through the sky it could take several thousand images automatically. These showed everything on the ground below, covering a strip of land 3,500 kilometres long and 200 kilometres wide. The pictures from the camera were so sharp and so detailed that it was possible to spot something as small as a shoebox from about 20 kilometres away.

The CIA had told the US government that it wasn't possible for the Soviet military to track a U-2 because it flew too high to show up on their radar. However, it soon became clear that this wasn't true, and in May 1956 the Russians spotted something entering their airspace. Luckily for the CIA, the Russians didn't know what they were looking at on their screens, and the Americans immediately denied that they had any military aircraft in the area.

Strictly speaking, this was true. The CIA was a civilian organisation rather than a part of the American military, but the Americans must have been worried. President Eisenhower didn't want American voters finding out that `their country was breaking the law`, and he certainly didn't want to start a third world war against the huge and heavily armed Soviet Union.

On the other hand, the U-2's pilot had managed to take lots of very useful photographs of Moscow, the Russian capital. He had also flown over several secret airbases and missile sites, so permission was given for the illegal flights to continue. This infuriated the Russians, but they were too embarrassed to say much about it publicly because this would have meant admitting they didn't have any aeroplanes that could fly high enough to shoot down the mysterious intruder.

Many ordinary Americans might have found this amusing, except that none of them knew about the U-2 spy plane either. Incredibly, it took almost four years before anybody could get close enough to one to take a photograph. Even then, the photographer who did manage it

(he was an Israeli fighter pilot) had no idea what it was.

All this was about to change, however. By 1960 the CIA had managed to photograph more than 3,000,000 square kilometres of enemy territory and compiled at least 5,500 secret intelligence reports on the country, its people and its weapons. Although Eisenhower knew that Russian anti-aircraft technology had improved dramatically since the first U-2 flight, he agreed to allow one more mission in order to spy on several strategically important missile, nuclear and submarine bases.

The pilot chosen for this task was called Francis Gary Powers. He was one of the CIA's most experienced airmen, but this time the Russians were ready for him. They spotted his U-2 before it was even inside Russian airspace and launched three surface-to-air missiles once Powers had crossed over the border. All three missed their target, but one of them exploded close enough to the aircraft to bring it down.

The Americans were sure that no one could survive a crash from a height of 21,000 metres. They assumed that Powers was dead and quickly issued a fake news story about an innocent scientific research flight that had got into trouble over Turkey. In fact, the Russians already had Powers in captivity and had been delighted to find all of the CIA's top-secret equipment on board the badly damaged U-2. As well as the amazing camera, this included a special 'suicide coin' for the pilot which contained a pin coated in deadly poison.

Now it was America's turn to be embarrassed, but Eisenhower refused to apologise for the incident or even to agree to cancel future U-2 flights. Powers was promptly put on trial, and after admitting he was a spy was sentenced to ten years in prison. Surprisingly, he was freed after only twenty-one months behind bars, but the episode was a catastrophe in terms of America's reputation around the world.

Suddenly, everyone knew about the U-2s and the illegal CIA missions. The Russians were now able to begin building their own spy planes by studying the wreckage and the remains of the Hycon camera. And after agreeing to send Powers back to the US, Russia managed to secure the freedom of one of their best agents, who had been sentenced to thirty years in prison in the US.

Powers continued flying after his return to America, initially as a test pilot for Lockheed. Some Americans called him a coward and a traitor because he had apologised to the Russians, but for many others he is still considered to be a genuine Cold War hero.

Yuri Gagarin

The First Man in Space (Russia, 1961)

As well as attack and defence, the Cold War was about national pride and new technology. Because of this, the so-called Space Race between Russia and America formed an important part of it.

Several countries had used rockets as weapons during World War II, but the most advanced ones had been developed in Germany. Following Hitler's defeat in 1945, the Russians and Americans were so desperate to acquire secret information about their technology that thousands of German scientists and rocket engineers were kidnapped and transported out of the country. Many of them were Nazis who should have been tried for war crimes. (German V-2 rockets were built using slave labour and killed huge numbers of innocent men, women and children.) Instead, the best specialists were given well-paid jobs designing new and better rockets for their old enemies.

The result was some truly remarkable achievements in science and technology, because

rockets have many other uses besides killing people. Both Russia and America wanted to build weapons based on the Germans' knowledge and expertise, but they were also interested in exploring the solar system. Many of the scientists were put to work developing intercontinental ballistic missiles (or ICBMs), a new type of weapon that could be fired at a target from thousands of kilometres away. But others looked to the stars, and their work quickly led to the launch of Sputnik, the world's first-ever man-made satellite.

Sputnik was a small aluminium sphere about 55 centimetres in diameter. It was blasted into orbit by Russia in October 1957, although it couldn't do much when it got there except make bleeping noises. These could be picked up by radios back on Earth, although the Russian leader Nikita Khrushchev wasn't very impressed by this and went straight back to bed after being woken up and told about it. However, the Americans were horrified when they heard the news. Many thought they had lost the Space Race before it had even really got going.

Two months later the US tried to launch a small satellite of its own, but the rocket exploded just four feet from the ground and the project was immediately given the nickname 'Flopnik' by journalists. Now the race got really serious as embarrassed American politicians realised they needed to spend hundreds of millions of dollars to make sure that they would eventually beat the Russians.

People around the world found the idea of these satellites exciting to begin with, and today we rely on them for the internet, weather forecasts and the navigation apps in our cars and mobile phones, among other things. More than thirty different ones had been launched by 1960, including one carrying a dog called Laika. Various little monkeys, frogs, mice, a rabbit and even some insects and plants followed Laika into space, but what everyone really wanted was for a human being to orbit the Earth.

Both America and Russia were soon spending a fortune on projects designed to achieve this. These were code-named Mercury and Vostok respectively, and once again it was a Russian who rocketed into the lead.

Yuri Gagarin was the son of a carpenter and worked in a steel factory before joining a flying club and then the air force. As a teenager he learned to fly in an old-fashioned, canvas-covered biplane, and less than a decade later he found himself sitting in a nearly 40-metre-tall Vostok-1 rocket, waiting to be fired into space.

Gagarin himself was only 1.57 metres tall, so his flying instructor had given him a cushion to sit on to help him see out of the biplane's cockpit. Later, when the Russians were looking for someone to send into space, `his height turned out to be an important advantage` because the cabin of the Vostok spacecraft was so small and cramped.

More than 150 of Russia's top fighter pilots were competing to be chosen, and all of them went through months of special training. This included being starved of oxygen to see how they would react if anything went wrong with the spacecraft, and then spending nearly two weeks alone in a special soundproof isolation chamber.

Just four days after being told that he had beaten the others, Russia's first cosmonaut strapped himself into his seat and got ready for take-off. Gagarin had hardly slept the night before, and he hadn't shaved because Russian pilots think this is unlucky. However, he sounded cheerful and optimistic, saying, 'Off we go! Goodbye until we meet soon, dear friends,' immediately before his four rocket motors roared dramatically into life and the historic flight began.

As the rocket rose through the air Gagarin's body was subjected to enormous pressures, and his heart rate rose alarmingly. This made it hard for him to speak, and for around five minutes the silence made it seem as though his radio was actually broken. Down on the ground there was an agonising wait – no one knew what was going on. Then a few words of Russian were heard over the radio's crackle and hiss. 'I see Earth,' a delighted Gagarin was saying. 'I see the clouds. It's beautiful.'

The Vostok had travelled barely more than 150 kilometres at this point, but after more than 300,000 years of human life on Earth no one had ever seen what its pilot could see now. Eventually reaching just over twice this altitude and a maximum speed of 27,400 kph,

the capsule and its precious cargo went once around the world before re-entering the atmosphere. Having made the first-ever manned orbit of our planet, Gagarin parachuted back down to the ground.

The spacecraft had been supplied with enough food and water for ten days in case anything went wrong, but Gagarin's flight had lasted a total of just 108 minutes. No one cared that he had failed to make any notes during the flight (unfortunately, his pencil had drifted off in the weightless conditions and got lost) or that the Vostok capsule had landed hundreds of kilometres off target. All that mattered was that a man had travelled into space and come home safely.

Staff at NASA (America's National Aeronautics and Space Administration) were shocked to discover they had been beaten, and the Russians were naturally overjoyed to have come first yet again. Hundreds of thousands turned out to see their smiling hero when he arrived in Moscow's Red Square, and `Yuri Gagarin's name was soon one of the most famous in the world`.

NASA wasn't about to give up, though. Less than a month later astronaut Alan Shepard became the first American in space. By 1963, when Russia's Valentina Tereshkova became the first woman, thousands of American scientists, mathematicians and engineers were already working hard to achieve their president's promise that humans would soon walk on the surface of the Moon.

Alan Pollock

A Birthday Surprise for London (England, 1968)

Britain at this time managed to launch only one small satellite into orbit using a British-made rocket, but 1968 was still an important year for British aviation. It marked the fiftieth anniversary of the world's first independent air force.

The RAF had been established on 1 April 1918 as a separate organisation rather than as part of the army or Royal Navy. There were no plans to celebrate its creation half a century later, not even by giving everyone a half-day holiday. This was all to save money, and it upset many pilots. One of them was Flight Lieutenant Alan Pollock, a member of No. 1 Squadron – the RAF's oldest – who wanted to commemorate the more than 70,000 RAF personnel who had been killed fighting for their country.

Pollock was an outstanding pilot who had served in Germany and the Middle East. He was also a bit of a showman and had a trick of flying his Hawker Hunter jet upside down and so low that the tail fin almost scraped along the runway. He had an idea,

and during a routine flight with three other Hunters from an airfield in Sussex to their base in Norfolk, he decided to veer off and head for central London.

Pollock's plan was to fly his camouflaged fighter extremely low over 10 Downing Street and the Houses of Parliament. He had decided to wake the MPs up, to remind them that the country had an air force worth celebrating. This would involve flying east into London along the River Thames and then onwards, twisting and turning as he passed three large war memorials on the river's northern bank. These are still there today and commemorate the RAF, the Fleet Air Arm and the Battle of Britain.

The first part of the plan went perfectly, and as Big Ben chimed 12 o'clock Pollock circled the Houses of Parliament three times, before pointing his jet's nose back down the river. Unfortunately, he had forgotten that Tower Bridge blocked his route out of London and that the world-famous stone and steel structure was so much taller than the other bridges over the Thames.

The Hunter could easily have flown over the historic landmark, but in a split-second decision Pollock made up his mind to fly *through* it instead. **He shot beneath the raised walkways at a speed of more than 650 kph**, a stunt which startled the passengers on a red double-decker which was crossing at that moment. According to one newspaper report, the thunderous roar from the Hunter's powerful Rolls-Royce engine also surprised a man on a bicycle and he promptly fell off.

Understandably, not everyone enjoyed Pollock's spectacular manoeuvre as much as he did. A boatman on the Thames thought he was dreaming, and various politicians and senior figures in the RAF were clearly furious. Many of them wanted to see Pollock punished, and the police arrested him not long after he had landed his Hunter in Norfolk and climbed down from the cockpit. As an officer he would almost certainly have faced a court martial (a type of military trial) and then been sacked, except that many members of the public supported what he had done and seemed to applaud his reasons for doing it.

Different newspapers described Pollock as both a hero and a hooligan, and this put the RAF in a difficult position. On the one hand, the whole thing had been a dangerous stunt, and could have been a disastrous one. The Hunter's wings and tail fin must have come within metres of hitting the bridge, and Pollock had clearly broken all sorts of regulations. On the other hand, no damage had been done, except to the cyclist's trousers. No one had been injured either, and people walking along the river at the time had clearly enjoyed seeing the stunning Hunter and one of the RAF's top pilots demonstrating his flying skills in such a dramatic and unique fashion.

Officials at the Ministry of Defence also wanted to avoid giving Pollock the opportunity to go on television and explain why he had done what he did. Some members of the government were embarrassed about the lack of any proper anniversary celebrations and worried that Pollock might cause a political scandal if he spoke out about it.

Fortunately for them, Pollock fell ill with a chest infection. He was hospitalised and immediately received hundreds of get-well cards from members of the public. While the other pilots in his squadron were sent to North Africa on a weapons training exercise, Pollock was ordered to stay behind to recover. A few weeks later he was well again, but it was quietly announced that he would be retiring from the RAF for medical reasons.

What the newspapers called the 'Tower Bridge incident' seemed to be over, but it was never entirely forgotten. Although it's true that it had cost a talented pilot his flying career, the Ministry of Defence made sure never to overlook an important military anniversary again. In 1982 Pollock was officially cleared of any wrongdoing, and in 2018, when the RAF celebrated its centenary, **more than a hundred different aircraft** flew in formation over Buckingham Palace. Tens of thousands of spectators cheered them from the streets below, and at airfields up and down the country Flight Lieutenant Alan Pollock's name – and his unusual tribute to his fellow pilots – was recalled with pride.

Concorde

Fast, Faster, Fastest (UK/France, 1969)

The success of jet airliners meant that by the 1960s passengers could travel to new destinations all over the world, and in less time than ever before. A flight from London to New York that would have taken fifteen hours in the 1950s could be made in less than half the time a decade later. These long-distance flights were still expensive, but prices gradually came down, allowing more and more people to experience the excitement of flying off on a foreign holiday.

Many of these jets flew at nearly 1,000 kph, compared to the 600 kph maximum speed of their older, propeller-driven rivals. But then, in March 1969, a team of British and French engineers unveiled something completely new – and extremely exciting. Its first flight lasted just half an hour, but everyone who saw the news film of Concorde taking off in France could see straight away how different it was to anything that had flown before.

It looked very different, with its huge triangular, or 'delta', wings and a sharply pointed nose that could be angled downwards for taking off and landing. It also sounded different thanks to four immense Rolls-Royce Olympus jets, which had been developed from the engines that powered the TSR-2, one of the most advanced combat aircraft of the entire Cold War era. Easily the most powerful engines of their kind in the world, they gave Concorde **a top speed of almost 2,200 kph**, or more than twice the speed of sound.

Concorde immediately revolutionised air travel and its arrival meant that anyone could now fly faster than a fighter pilot. Anyone who could afford it, that is, because everything about this sleek and spectacular machine was expensive. It wasn't just the tickets – although when they went on sale these cost seven or eight times as much as normal ones – but also the aeroplanes themselves.

Britain and France had calculated that a small fleet of Concordes would cost around £150 million to design and get airborne. In fact, the final cost of the fleet was almost £2 *billion*, which is the main reason why the US president quickly cancelled his country's plans to build a supersonic rival of its own.

Concorde was also incredibly expensive to fly. It needed thirteen gigantic fuel tanks, even though it carried fewer passengers than an ordinary airliner, each aircraft consuming more than 25,000 litres of fuel an hour when it was airborne. That's the same amount a normal family-sized car would need to drive all the way around the world ten or even twelve times.

Concorde also burned another two tonnes of fuel just getting from the airport terminal to the runway, so the carbon footprint of even a single flight was horrendous.

Its engines produced three times as much carbon dioxide and other greenhouse gases as those of any modern jet, and their poisonous emissions were at least five times as damaging to the environment because Concorde flew at a much higher altitude. They were also so much noisier than ordinary jet engines (even at 18,000 metres) that pilots were allowed to fly at supersonic speeds only when they were far out over the sea. `Concorde's sonic boom would have broken windows 100 kilometres` away had they been permitted to fly this fast over land, so perhaps it's not surprising that many countries simply banned the aircraft from flying over their territory. In the end only two airlines decided to buy the plane (one British and one French), and neither made a profit.

Despite these problems, however, most people at the time agreed that Concorde was a truly beautiful creation, and more than fifty years after that first flight it still looks like a machine from the future.

Perhaps because it caused such a sensation, hardly anyone was worried about the pollution and environmental damage caused by travelling this fast. No one seemed to care that its graceful, slim shape meant that the narrow, noisy cabin was more cramped than other aeroplanes. And no one minded that the deep-blue leather seats were less spacious than the ones found in the first-class section of normal airliners and had far less leg room.

This was true even though Concorde actually stretched by up to 25 centimetres when it was flying due to the heat generated by travelling more than a mile through the air every three seconds. Instead, the rich and famous queued up to fly across the world in supersonic style. Queen Elizabeth II travelled on Concorde several times, her husband Prince Philip once actually took the controls, and even those who could afford only to watch it streaking across the sky told each other it was one of the most magnificent machines ever created.

For aviation engineers it was a genuine technological masterpiece, the result of more than five million miles' worth of test flights and an incredible 2,000 hours spent flying at supersonic speeds. For politicians Concorde also symbolised the successful co-operation of two European countries, and it quickly became a source of `great national pride in both Britain and France`.

For its passengers, however, Concorde was something altogether more magical. For the first time ever, ordinary men and women could fly not only faster than fighter pilots but so high that (like astronauts) they could look down and see the gradual curve of our planet's surface. The five-hour time difference between Europe and America also meant that by cutting transatlantic journey times to under three hours, those same passengers could arrive at their destination earlier in the day than when they had taken off.

Unfortunately, in 2000 a disastrous crash involving an Air France Concorde killed everyone on board. This brought the whole supersonic era to a sudden end, but by then Concorde had

made 50,000 flights, spent more time at supersonic speeds than all the world's air forces combined and carried a total of 2.5 million passengers. One of them, a man called Fred, travelled on it an astonishing 718 times (he always sat in seat number 9A), and over the years its passengers are estimated to have drunk around a million bottles of Champagne.

Happily, eighteen of these beautiful aircraft still exist and are now in museums or on public display. As nothing similar has been built (not yet anyway), this means that once again, more than half a century after Concorde's first momentous appearance on the runway, the only way to fly at the speed of sound is to join the air force – or become an astronaut.

The Saturn V Rockets

Walking on the Moon (Outer Space, 1969)

The Americans had been deeply shocked when Russia beat them to launch the first-ever satellite into orbit, and then in 1961 the first human being. The year after Yuri Gagarin's pioneering journey, the US president made a famous speech to cheer them up. John F. Kennedy announced that America would be the first country to put a man on the Moon, and that it would do so before the end of the decade.

Not everyone believed it was possible, and more than half of Americans didn't even think it was a good idea. Other politicians complained about how much the Space Race was costing the country, and scientists were worried about the dangers. But the president was determined to push ahead with what became known as the Apollo missions. Kennedy was convinced a moon landing would be good for science and that beating the Russians would be good for American morale. He was probably right, but can't have known how hard it would be to achieve this goal.

The numbers tell us all we need to know. So far, more than 5,000 rockets have been launched into space and approximately 600 men and women from dozens of different countries have travelled on them. But only twelve of them have been lucky enough to stand on the Moon's surface and look back at our beautiful blue-green planet.

The reason for this is that getting even a small number of astronauts there and back safely turned out to be so difficult and so dangerous that Apollo expanded to become the single most expensive engineering project in history. More than 400,000 people and 20,000 companies and universities worked for years to make it possible. This involved designing and building the world's most powerful, most complicated machines, and it cost the US the equivalent of more than £170 billion.

The machines were the fabulous Saturn V rockets, and their mission couldn't have been more exciting. They were designed to make the longest journey in the whole of human history and to enable our species – for the very first time – to step off its own world and on to another one.

An incredible mission needs incredible rockets, and the Saturn Vs are still the most incredible ones ever built. A world championship-winning Formula 1 car has about 25,000 parts, which sounds like a lot until you compare it to a Saturn V. It had approximately three million different components, and every one of them had to be specially designed and built from scratch.

The result wasn't just more powerful than any previous rocket but also much larger. Saturn Vs were 111 metres long from end to end, and at 2.8 million kilogrammes heavier than twenty blue whales. In fact, they were so much taller than both New York's Statue of Liberty and the tower we call Big Ben that one of the first things NASA had to do was construct a brand-new factory in Florida that was large enough to contain them.

The factory is called the Vehicle Assembly Building (VAB), and it is still one of the most extraordinary structures anywhere in the world. Its roof is so high that rain clouds sometimes form inside it, and the four main doors are the largest ones ever made. They take forty-five minutes just to open or close, and the space inside is so enormous that you could fit nearly 10,000 ordinary school classrooms into it.

The rockets built there are still some of the largest and heaviest ones ever launched. Despite this, each of the 2,800-tonne giants could carry only three people at a time. The crew sat squashed inside a tiny capsule at the top called the command module. Nearly the whole of the rest of the rocket was taken up by eleven of the most powerful engines ever produced and the huge quantity of fuel needed to travel nearly 800,000 kilometres through space.

The Saturn V carried something else in it too, though, which was another, smaller spaceship called the lunar module. Once the crew got close enough to the Moon, two of the three astronauts used this to fly the last 110 kilometres down to its surface and then to take off again once they were ready to leave.

Americans were naturally excited about the possibility of a Moon landing, but so were people from all over the world. In July 1969 more than half a billion of them switched on their televisions to watch the crew of Apollo 11 climbing into the capsule. Even more surprising is that nearly a million others actually travelled to the launch site at Cape Canaveral. It seemed like everyone on Earth wanted to see Neil Armstrong, Buzz Aldrin and Peter Collins taking off.

Rockets go wrong all the time, so these spectators were ordered to keep several kilometres away from the launch pad in case this one exploded. Happily, nothing bad happened, but even at this distance the sound was deafening as the first five motors ignited in a blaze of burning light and thick black smoke.

People living in the area felt the ground shake like an earthquake as the Saturn V rose into the air. The lift-off was slow at first, and then things started happening incredibly fast. A staggering 3.5 million litres of kerosene, hydrogen and oxygen were needed to launch the crew beyond the pull of Earth's gravity. In the first second the Saturn V consumed nearly ten times as much fuel as Charles Lindbergh's aircraft had needed to cross the Atlantic, and almost all the rest was gone in the first few minutes.

Very soon the Saturn V was too high to see, and in under three hours Armstrong, Aldrin and Collins were already orbiting the Earth. Most of the now-empty rocket had been left behind to burn up in the atmosphere or crash down into the sea. Only the tip of it was needed to fly more than a third of a million kilometres to the Moon, and an even smaller part of it was all that would return to Earth eight days later, with the three men strapped inside.

Between the launch and the Moon landing, hundreds of millions of viewers sat glued to their television screens watching as the three men travelled at almost 40,000 kph through the cold, dark silence of space. The crew spent almost the entire journey in the tiny capsule, but then about a hundred hours into the mission Armstrong and Aldrin began preparing to clamber from the command module into the lunar module. While Collins remained in orbit around the Moon, his companions commenced their historic flight down to the surface.

It's impossible to say which part of Apollo 11's journey was the most dangerous, but this was certainly one of them. Until now much of the mission had been controlled by huge computers, but now all of Armstrong's skills as a top US Navy test pilot were needed to ensure the fragile lunar module made a safe landing on this unknown world.

As they neared the surface the two men realised their landing site was covered with boulders. Some were as large as cars and could easily have wrecked their craft, so Armstrong spent the last few seconds skilfully flying over these towards a better spot. He later described this as his favourite part of the mission, although it meant that by the time they landed there was only just enough fuel left to take off again when it was time to return to Collins and the capsule.

The first few steps on the Moon represented a giant leap forward for both technology and humankind. The Americans' success was one of the most important episodes in the history of flight, but it was also an incredible achievement for humanity. A bit like the Wright brothers' flight sixty-six years earlier, it was also surprisingly short. The two men spent less than a day on the surface before rejoining Collins and flying home. Ten other astronauts followed in their footsteps (as part of another five Apollo missions), but by 1972 it was all over. More than half a century later no one else has ever been back to the Moon to stand on its surface and wave back at Earth.

The Northrop-Grumman B-2 Spirit

Now You See Us, Now You Don't (US, 1977)

Rocket technology was improving very fast by the 1970s. Missiles could fly thousands of miles across entire continents by remote control, and unmanned aeroplanes called drones began to play a significant role in modern warfare. However, piloted aircraft were still important to the military, so to improve the protection of crew members a number of different methods were tried.

A very few aircraft flew so fast that missiles couldn't catch them. America's SR-71 Blackbird spy plane, for example, was designed to travel at more than three times the speed of sound. Its exact top speed is still a closely guarded secret, but it is certainly more than 3,500 kph – or nearly 60 kilometres per minute.

The Americans also experimented with devices called 'parasite fighters', which were so small they could be carried inside much larger nuclear bombers. If the bomber was attacked, one of these tiny fighters would fly out from beneath its body and shoot down the attacker. This experiment was not successful, and flying higher and higher didn't work very well either. Something else was needed to protect air force pilots from attack, and it arrived in 1977.

The new technology grew out of another secret project at Lockheed's mysterious Skunk Works factory. Lockheed's code name for it was Have Blue, and it was an attempt to build an aircraft which simply didn't show up on normal radar screens. This would make it possible for the Americans to attack an enemy target without warning, a bit like Russia's World War II Night Witches did by switching off their engines. Pilots could also make their getaway before anyone on the ground realised what was happening.

Obviously, it wasn't possible to build an aircraft which was actually invisible, so Lockheed's engineers began devising something called 'stealth' technology. This was designed to make an aeroplane flying at night `almost impossible to detect`, even by using the most advanced surveillance equipment, such as radar, which makes it possible to spot an ordinary aircraft or missile from hundreds of kilometres away.

Radar works by sending radio waves into the sky like invisible beams of energy. If these hit an object such as an aeroplane, they are reflected or bounced back to the radar station. A skilful radar operator can then work out what the object is and calculate how fast it is flying

and in what direction.

Stealth technology is designed to cheat the radar and confuse the operator by using a combination of strange shapes, special paint and sophisticated new materials called composites. The strangely angled shapes of stealth aircraft bounce the invisible beams off in all directions instead of straight back to the radar station. Special paints absorb some of the radio waves rather than reflecting them, and lightweight materials (like the carbon fibre used in modern Formula 1 cars) make the aircraft harder to detect on radar than if they were constructed using ordinary metals such as aluminium, magnesium and steel. The combined effect of all this is to trick the radar into thinking it is 'seeing' something else, often something much smaller than an aeroplane or missile. This gives the pilot an opportunity to launch a surprise attack, which is an enormous advantage in nearly all combat missions.

This sort of know-how is now being applied to ships and even tanks, but the most extraordinary and advanced examples of stealth technology are still certain types of fighter and bomber aircraft. The Northrop-Grumman B-2 Spirit, for example, is **the most expensive aeroplane ever built**. Each one is estimated to have cost more than $2 billion. That's about £1.5 billion, or the same as four of the largest, most luxurious airliners in the world. This explains why just twenty-one have ever been completed, even though the US Air Force originally asked the American government to pay for 132 of them. Today there are only twenty of them in service because one crashed in 2008 shortly

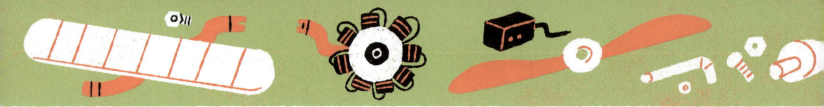

after taking off. It was completely destroyed, but fortunately both pilots escaped by ejecting moments before the aircraft hit the ground and burst into flames.

They look spectacular but highly unusual because the B-2 is another flying-wing design. Like the German Horten which caught fire and crashed in 1944, they don't have vertical tail fins or a cylindrical fuselage. Instead, everything on board a B-2 is carried inside the wing. This includes two crew members, nearly 100,000 litres of fuel and 18 tonnes of weapons.

The aircraft's curved shape and special non-reflective paint function so well that on an enemy's radar screen the B-2 looks no larger than a pigeon. In fact, **it weighs more than 150 tonnes** and has a wingspan of 52 metres, which is larger than that of many airliners.

Although the B-2 is not particularly fast, it can fly at more than 15 kilometres above sea level. This is higher than most aircraft and makes it harder to spot from the ground. The crew have no guns to defend themselves, but the bat-winged bomber has special 'stand-off' missiles that enable it to fire at a target from more than 100 kilometres away. This means the crew can launch an attack from a safe distance and turn for home before their enemies even know they are being attacked. Remarkably, a B-2 can also fly more than 11,000 kilometres without refuelling, which is equivalent to crossing the Atlantic Ocean twice.

However, the technology needed to do all this is so complicated that the B-2's running costs

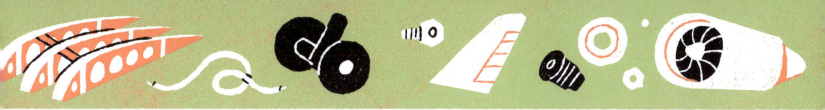

are enormous. It's been estimated that to fly it for just an hour costs £100,000. To make matters worse, every hour in the air requires nearly 120 hours of maintenance on the ground as soon as it lands. The aircraft also have to be housed in special air-conditioned hangars to prevent the expensive radar-absorbing paint from being damaged. All this means that each B-2 costs approximately £2.5 million a month to look after, which means the US Air Force spends well over £500 million a year keeping all twenty of them ready for action.

Despite these drawbacks, the B-2 holds the record for completing the longest air-combat mission in history. In 2001 six of them flew on a raid from the US to Afghanistan and back again, an achievement which required the crews to remain airborne and alert to danger for an incredible seventy hours without a break. While off duty, the B-2's distinctive shape has also enabled it to become a genuine Hollywood star, and several of them can be seen in hit movies such as *Iron Man 2*, *Captain Marvel* and *Armageddon*.

SpaceShipOne

Joyrides to the Stars (US, 2003)

In 1992 Concorde set a new record by flying around the world in less than thirty-one hours. Its four famously thirsty engines meant the French crew had to stop and refuel no fewer than six times, unlike a very different kind of aircraft which had done the same thing six years earlier. In 1986 pilots Dick Rutan and Jeana Yeager completed the same journey without landing even once. To do so they had to stay airborne for nine days, three minutes and forty-four seconds – a very different kind of record to Concorde's but one which is just as impressive.

Their aircraft, the Voyager, isn't as beautiful as Concorde or as comfortable, and obviously it is nowhere near as fast. But in at least one way it now looks like a more important machine. While Concorde managed to cut the time taken to fly to America, the flight of the Voyager paved the way for even more people to travel out into space.

One of the things that makes the Voyager so remarkable is its weight: at only 1,020 kilogrammes it weighs a lot less than even a small car like the Mini or Fiat 500. The use of advanced new materials such as carbon fibre and Kevlar instead of metal mean its body and wings are incredibly strong but also very light. As a result Yeager and Rutan used much less fuel than an ordinary aeroplane would have needed to complete the same 42,432-kilometre journey. This made the non-stop journey possible, but also dramatically reduced its impact on the environment. Unfortunately, conventional jet aircraft are so polluting that scientists have calculated that if the aviation industry were a country, it would be the tenth dirtiest on the planet in terms of greenhouse gases.

The pollution from aircraft has been getting worse for years because more and more people are flying than ever before. For a while it looked as though new types of aircraft, like the Voyager, might be a solution, because the most effective way to cut harmful emissions is to use less fuel. Lighter aircraft would have made this possible, except that the team behind Voyager decided to use the same technology to build spacecraft instead.

In 2003 the company launched SpaceShipOne and made the first-ever privately funded human space flight when pilot Mike Melvill reached a height of 100 kilometres. That's far lower than the altitude needed to go into orbit, but the flight was still an important milestone and the company was rewarded with a generous **$10 million prize for innovation**.

Before this all space flights had been funded by national governments rather than by companies or private individuals. The American astronauts and Russian cosmonauts who

travelled on them were also trained to carry out important scientific research rather than just enjoying themselves and looking at the view.

SpaceShipOne changed all that. The technology behind the project was brilliant, and Melvill was clearly a skilled and courageous pilot. But his flight shifted the focus away from science and exploration for the first time. Instead, people began to talk about space tourism and the exciting possibility that **ordinary people might soon be able to leave Earth** themselves instead of just watching others doing it on television.

By 2021 at least three different companies had built their own rockets designed to carry passengers, and another one announced that it was building a luxury hotel in space with room for several hundred guests. Naturally, anyone who wanted to experience any of this would have to be very well off or know someone rich enough to buy them a ticket.

One wealthy customer paid more than £20 million for his ticket, but these space tourists weren't astronauts in any real sense. One of the rockets went up only 80 kilometres (which many experts think doesn't really qualify as space travel), and in some cases the flights lasted just a few minutes. The people lucky enough to travel on them were really just passengers or joy-riders paying for a modern version of the 'five-bob flip' in a biplane that the barnstormers had offered spectators in the 1920s.

Despite this, the idea of day trips and even holidays in space is hugely exciting, but the ticket price isn't the only problem associated with this new kind of space race. There's also the huge environmental cost to consider, especially as the pollution it causes is set to rocket as more and more people join the queue to fly.

Each passenger on an ordinary airliner is responsible for producing the equivalent of three tonnes of carbon dioxide on a single long-haul flight. That's several times more than the average person in South America or Africa produces in an entire year, which is one of the reasons environmental campaigners want everyone to fly much less in future. You can double that amount for a return journey, but rockets are still far worse than aeroplanes. Every launch has an enormous carbon footprint, and toxic emissions at high altitude can hang around for years, making them much more damaging than those closer to the ground. In fact, a single rocket produces hundreds of tonnes of pollution at every launch – between five and ten times as much as Britain's dirtiest power station – and up to a hundred times more CO_2 per passenger than an airliner crossing the Atlantic.

This problem may not seem too serious today, when rocket launches are still relatively uncommon. However, one of the companies is planning to operate 400 flights a year for tourists, and when this happens the results could be catastrophic for the planet. Despite this, humans aren't about to abandon space travel, so we can only hope these rocket companies start looking soon for a cleaner and more sustainable way of reaching for the stars.

Epilogue

Going Green

Although no one is even thinking about building a 'green' rocket yet, the aviation industry is slowly beginning to explore different ideas for reducing the damaging environmental impact of more than 100,000 passenger and cargo flights every single day.

Human power still isn't practical, which is a shame because an aircraft one could pedal like a bicycle would probably be the greenest solution, if only it could be made to work. A handful of ultra-light, pedal-powered prototypes have managed to fly for a few minutes, but they all need long, fragile wings to do so and a very fit pilot who can pedal furiously, fly safely and navigate all at the same.

Incredibly, one of them, the *Gossamer Albatross*, succeeded in crossing the English Channel like Louis Blériot, a distance of just over 36 kilometres, but most manage only a few seconds in the air before coming down much like Brother Elmer did in the twelfth century. The others are really just gliders and have struggled to fly higher than two or three metres.

Talented designers and engineers have experimented with solar power as well, but this also works only for ultra-light aircraft, and so far none of them has had room for anyone other than the pilot. The most impressive examples are *Solar Impulse 1* and *Solar Impulse 2*. Their wings are covered in thousands of photovoltaic cells that generate electricity from the Sun, which is then stored in battery packs. Each could fly for several hours at a time, although they cost well over £100 million to build. They also needed enormous wingspans, making them even wider than an Airbus A340. An Airbus can carry nearly 400 passengers at a time, but neither *Solar Impulse* had enough room even for the pilot's hand baggage.

Electricity is also what powers Rolls-Royce's *Spirit of Innovation*, another single-seater. This one looks and flies much more like a conventional aeroplane, and in 2021 it climbed to an altitude of 3,000 metres. Its batteries produce enough electricity to power 7,500 mobile phones and enabled it to set a new electric speed world record of 623 kph.

Sadly, even this technology is still years away from being able to power a passenger airliner, and anyway batteries use up scarce resources and electric planes (like electric cars) make sense only if the electricity is generated cleanly and sustainably. Very often it isn't, but then the history of aviation includes many examples of machines which were impractical yet inspirational (this book is full of them!) and many stories of dreamers who failed but still managed to inspire others to succeed.

Clearly, the answer is to WATCH THIS SPACE, because whatever happens next in aviation, it definitely won't be boring.